INCOME FOR LIFE
for Canadians

How You Can Achieve Financial Freedom With This Proven Real Estate Investment System

Authors:
Tom Karadza
Nick Karadza
Rob Minton

Tom Karadza and Nick Karadza are licensed Real Estate Brokerss in Ontario, Canada. Tom Karadza and Nick Karadza are not licensed attorneys, lawyers, tax advisors, or any other licensed professionals. Anyone considering implementing these ideas and plans are advised to seek professional advice concerning legal and tax matters.

Robert Minton is a licensed Real Estate Broker in the state of Ohio. Robert Minton is not a licensed attorney, tax advisor, or any other licensed professional. Anyone considering implementing these ideas and plans are advised to seek professional advice concerning legal and tax matters.

Copyright © 2008 Rob Minton, Nick Karadza, Tom Karadza

Examples Updated January 2013.

No part of this book may be reproduced, stored in a retrieval system, or transmitted by any means without the written permission of the author and co-author.

ISBN: 978-1-4276-2866-4

Printed in Canada

I'd like to dedicate this book to the great mentors that have pushed me.

-Tom Karadza

I'd like to dedicate this book to all the people who have had a positive impact on my life. Your guidance has been invaluable.

-Nick Karadza

I'd like to dedicate this book to my family, team members, and investors. Without their support, I could have never done it.

-Rob Minton

Contents

1. Are You Ever Going to Be Able to Retire or Are You Going to Mop Floors at McDonalds? 1

2. How Not to Get Started! 9

3. A Simple SLOW Wealth Building Strategy 19

4. How $10,000 Can Make You Wealthy! The Buy & Hold Strategy Kicked Up a Notch 31

5. The 10/5/10 Investment Strategy 59

6. The MOST Important Key to Your Success in Real Estate Investing 69

7. How to Find & Buy Nice Homes Below Value 81

8. The 4 Point Home Search & How It Can Help You Buy Homes Below Value 95

9. How To Negotiate Thousands Off Of The Price When You Buy A Home 109

10. The Best Way to Market Your Home is to Advertise Three Magic Words <u>"Rent to Own"</u> 125

11. How to Show Your Home to Rent to Own Tenants ... 139

12. How You Can Make $48,321 on One Single-
Family Home in Your Spare Time ...………...……. 147

13. Investor Mistakes, Foul Ups & Blunders …………... 163

14. Will You or Won't You? That
is the Million Dollar Question...……… ……….……179

15. How You Can Create A Million Dollars For Your
Retirement Or Your Child's Financial Freedom ..…... 191

16. The Ultimate Investing Secret …….…………....…199

17. Do You Want to Guarantee YOUR Success? ...………207

Special Gift #1……………………………..……………......211

Special FREE Gift #2 …………………………......…….212

Special FREE Gift #3……………………………………….213

Contact the Authors …………………………….……….214
.
About the Authors …………………………….……...215

Introduction

We were standing in the parking lot of an Ohio Steak House when it hit me. I had driven from just outside Toronto to a small suburb in the U.S. to meet with someone who I had just learned about a couple of weeks earlier.

I won't drive 30 minutes to spend time with some of my own family. Why had I done driven all this way?

And then it became clear. A true leader will inspire you and that's what reading this book for the first time did to me. Throughout these pages Rob had finally laid down a detailed plan that I could follow. A blueprint, a system.

All the other real estate investing information that I had been exposed to was heavy on theory and concepts but light on real world application. This book changed that for me. Something finally clicked.

Although I had been investing in real estate prior to meeting Rob, the system he reveals in this book was eye opening.

Perhaps it is the stories in the pages ahead or the detailed numbers shared on the different investments. I still can't put my finger on it but I knew that I was reading a book written by a real investor. Not someone who was selling information. This was a person speaking from real and recent experiences.

Nick, my brother and business partner, and I quickly decided that we would bring the same step-by-step investing approach to Canada and we would share this book with as many people as possible.

It led to us working hand in hand with local investors to acquire over $290,000,000 worth of investment real estate that generates over $1,000,000 in gross monthly revenues.

To say that it has been life changing for hundreds of people would be an understatement.

Read and enjoy. Hopefully you will be inspired enough to take the next step on your real estate investing journey.

To Your Success,

Tom Karadza

1

Are You Ever Going to Be Able to Retire or
Are You Going to Mop Floors at McDonald's?

Have you ever walked into a fast food restaurant and noticed a Senior Citizen mopping the floors or cleaning the tables? I have, and it really breaks my heart. Do you think that the Senior Citizens who are mopping the floors dreamed of the day when they could retire and then work at McDonald's to earn some extra income? Can you picture them in their 20's, 30's, 40's and 50's just waiting for the day when they could start at McDonald's?

I am presenting this on the funny side, but it is a serious point for you to consider. The Senior Citizens you see working are not working because they want to. (Well, some of them probably do want to.) My mother retired a few years ago and has a part-time job because she likes to meet new people and see old friends at work! The majority of Senior Citizens are working because they have to. The reason they have to work is because their monthly income isn't enough to cover their monthly living expenses.

Do you want to mop floors and clean bathrooms when you hit your golden years? If not, then consider this:

If You Ever Want to Retire in Your Life, You Better Start to Create Passive Monthly Income Today

What is guaranteed to you in today's world? Is your job secure? Are you guaranteed to get Social Security or your pension at work? Will the stock market continue with hardly any growth? Study after study has shown that Social Security will run out of money. The reason is because the baby boomer population will go from working and paying to Social Security to retirement and collecting Social Security. The number of people still in the workforce paying into the plan will not be enough to cover all of the outgoing payments made to retirees.

Look at Enron! Thousands of employees' retirement accounts disappeared over night. Don't think that you will be safe. The biggest problem that I see most people make is to rely on one income. Relying on one of anything is very dangerous to you. If you are relying on your 401(k) or RRSP and the stock market crashes, you are going to suffer. If you are relying on Social Security and it runs out of money, you are going to suffer. In fact, many people rely on just one income from their job. What happens when the company downsizes and your one income goes away? Never rely on one of anything. It is far too risky.

You really need to protect yourself from the danger of "one" by creating other multiple income streams. By having 20 income streams coming to you each month, you are not as dependent on any one of them. This book is about building passive monthly income streams that you can live on to ensure your financial security and independence.

When I say passive income, I mean money that you receive every month from your investments. Understand that it takes some work to set up passive income streams. However, once your income streams are set up, you simply have to manage them.

In this book, I will show you how to create on average $58,004 in profits from buying just one single-family home for investment.

Let me ask you a very serious question:

If all you did was invest in two single-family homes and never did any other investing for the rest of your life, would you be better off financially?

Well, I know the answer and you know the answer. It's actually a silly question; however, the majority of people never ask themselves this question. If you kept your job and had two rental properties that would be three income streams you would have coming to you. As you will see shortly, it is actually many more income streams. Each income stream you create is added financial protection for you and your family.

What is the best investment your parents ever made? Many of you will say that your parents' best investment would have to be their homes. The next logical question then becomes, what would your parents' life look like, if they had bought two rental properties 30 years ago? What would the life of the Senior Citizen working at the fast food restaurant be like today had they invested in real estate earlier in their lives? Would they still be mopping the floors and cleaning ketchup off of the tables?

I don't want to see you cleaning floors; instead, my goal with this book is to motivate you to just invest in a few single-family homes. That's it. I know that if I can give you the encouragement and tools to get started, you can dramatically change your future. If you take the ideas in this book and continue to buy two homes a year for the next 10 years that would be fantastic! The focus is for you to get started today and build monthly passive income so that you can live life on your terms and not be dependent on any one income stream.

Think about this:

If you were to invest in just one single-family home today and keep it until your retirement, you would increase your net worth by $411,613. You would have a monthly income from this one home in excess of $1,330. (A $100,000 home appreciating at 5% a year for 30 years would be worth $411,613.) And that's a conservative example. It could be much more in a market experiencing larger appreciation or with higher price points.

Just a few homes purchased now could make you a millionaire in retirement. By owning real estate as an investment, you are not relying on Social Security or your employer's pension. If you are lucky enough to receive Social Security or a pension, super for you! Treat it as a bonus. However, by owning real estate, you are guaranteeing your future financial security and not just hoping for the best.

The amount of income you create from your real estate investing is completely up to you. In fact, how quickly you can achieve financial independence is entirely up to you too. One of my client members, Joe Mercadante, was able to achieve financial independence in seven months at the age of 34. You can create as much income, or as little as you want. The choice is 100% yours.

The reason I am able to say this so confidently is because I have some clients that only create $15,000 on one property and don't do anything else. I have other clients that create $30,000 on one property and then repeat the process over and over again on other properties.

You see, building your wealth is simple, but it's not easy. The thought of buying two homes and renting them out is simple. But actually doing it is not easy.

That's where this book comes in. This book will help you make the simple, easy!

Now for a strictly Canadian perspective...

A couple of excellent points have been brought up.

i) How many poor people do you know that own real estate as an investment?
ii) Real Estate investing is simple, but not easy (at first anyway).

When I ask family or friends what the best investment they have ever made the response is almost unanimous. Their home is by far and away their best investment.

If you then ask them if they have purchased just one more home as an investment, again, the answer is almost always the same. They have always thought about it but just haven't gotten around to it.

Who can blame them? The first house is purchased out of necessity. We all need shelter. It just so happens that the house that was purchased to put a roof of your head also turns out to be a great investment.

You are almost forced into the decision. Now there may still be fear in signing your first set of mortgage papers but there was motivation to go through with it.

So it's likely not a stretch to have you agree that a house is a great investment but the majority of the population doesn't take the next step and purchase a second one.

Why is it that most of us stop right there?

There are two main reasons:

i) Fear. Fear of the unknown, fear of losing money, fear of failure.
ii) Education. We have an education system that does not teach us about finances or financial independence.

As mentioned earlier in this chapter, investing in real estate is a simple process. Getting over your fears and taking the action required to do it is often not easy. At first anyway.

The only way to get through fear is to take action. The next few pages of this book will share strategies for investing in Real Estate that will help remove the fear.

With the right education in real estate investing your fear in taking the first step will fade.

Often retirees will comment to me that their lives would have been very different had they just invested in one more house.

There always seems to be a huge amount of regret in those words. Will that be you?

Get the education! Step through the fear!

Read on…

8

2

How Not to Get Started!

Before we get started in the nitty, gritty details, I thought I should share some background information on myself with you so that you might have a better understanding of how I approach real estate investing. I used to be a CPA with a large accounting firm and hated every minute of it. Every Sunday night, I would have a pit in my stomach with the thought of having to start another work week. My job in the accounting firm was to go audit our clients' financial statements. So every day I would go to work at companies that didn't really want me there. I was an auditor. Nobody likes an auditor.

While auditing these companies, I started to feel like I was on the sidelines watching them make things happen. My clients' companies were making things happen. They were in the game. I felt as if I weren't really in the game. I was just checking the score. Who likes to sit on the sidelines? The fun is in the game.

Ever since college, I knew that real estate investing was very profitable. I kept thinking that real estate investing would be a great way to earn a living without having to sit behind a desk all day long. So, like many people, I bought one of those so-called "get rich buying real estate" systems from a TV commercial. I won't name any names, but if you turn on your TV very late tonight, I would be willing to bet you will find a new version of the same commercial running on some channel. I read every book I could find on how to buy foreclosed homes and sell them for a profit. I can honestly say that I tried everything recommended from these books and tapes. This book has been written with my blood, sweat and tears of real estate investment. As an investor, I have learned from my own real life experiences. As a real estate broker, I have learned from countless clients that have invested in real estate using different approaches.

The approach to investing that we have moved toward over all of these years has been working so well because of the underlying philosophy, which I will explain in detail throughout this book. It took a lot of mistakes to realize why investing in real estate was so challenging. Here are some of my mistakes....

My First Try to Make Money...

I found out through the school of hard knocks that Get Rich in Your Spare Time really meant spending a whole lot of time making not so much money. One of the books that I read recommended that I go find sellers that would sell their home to me and act as the bank. So, in essence, I should buy their home and they would receive monthly payments from me over time instead of their full sales price at the time of sale. With this approach, I supposedly wouldn't need a bank and could buy homes without having a down payment. The truth was that the only people willing to accept this arrangement had homes that were garbage. In the late 1990's and early 2000's mortgage interest rates became so low that there has been a huge supply of home buyers. Because there are so many buyers, home sellers can get their full sales price without having to take any risk by accepting monthly payments. The real estate market in general over the last few years has been a seller's market. This means that in most cases the seller calls the shots. If interest rates go into the double digits again, I suspect that these techniques might be more profitable because the market will become a buyer's market.

My Second Try to Make Money…

My next approach to making money was to try to buy foreclosed homes and fix them up for a quick resale. Hey, wait a minute; on the TV commercial, these guys were making $50,000 or $60,000 in a weekend. So this seemed like a logical step in my investing career. So I ran out and got pre-approved for a mortgage. Then the foreclosure book told me to go to sheriff sales and make bids on foreclosed homes. So that is what I did. I spent the good part of a year looking for foreclosure homes. This entailed studying legal foreclosure notices, researching the public records, reviewing the foreclosure records at the court house, driving by and looking at the exterior of the foreclosed homes, going to the sheriff sales to bid on these homes. You notice that above I stated that I spent the good part of the year trying to profit from flipping foreclosed homes.

I invested nine months in this approach to real estate investing; except that when you invest, you typically get a return on your investment. In my case, I guess I didn't invest; I just burned the rubber off my tires. I spent nine months trying to bird dog these foreclosures without earning $1.00. During this whole time, I wasn't able to buy any of these foreclosed homes. What I found out is that in most cases, the lender/bank that is foreclosing on the home usually buys the home back at the sheriff sale. The lender's position is that they will make more money buying the home at the sheriff sale and then listing it for sale with a Realtor than if they let it sell at the auction. The reason is that they don't want some greedy investor, like you, to make all of the money. So on every occasion that I was bidding at a sheriff sale, my highest bid was outbid by the foreclosing lenders or someone else.

Quick Tip: If you are going to buy homes at an auction, you should consider not bidding at all during the auction. My suggestion would be to approach the winning bidder after the gavel drops and offer them a few thousand dollars more for the property. Using this method, the home's price doesn't get bid up too high and you get the home at a much lower price. You would buy the home directly from the winning bidder. The winning bidder gets to collect a few thousand dollars for a few minutes of their time!

Let's See the Math on This....

Now, I am pretty bad with numbers (joke), but how much do I have to earn on my first foreclosure deal to earn a profit? Let's figure this out together: Assume that I invested about 10 hours a week during those nine months, for a total of 360 hours. Now let's suppose that I was actually successful in buying one of these homes and I only needed to invest another 200 hours to manage the repairs, and market and show the home for the resale. I would have a total of 560 hours invested in making money with my lovely foreclosed home. If I were to do extremely well and make a profit of $10,000 on the home, my profit per hour would be $17.86. I guess that's not too bad if I don't consider the risk that the home wouldn't sell very quickly, which would mean that I would still have to pay the mortgage and all utilities and taxes during the whole marketing period.

Another big problem with trying to buy homes at the sheriff sales is that you cannot inspect the home before you make an offer. The reason is that prior to the auction day, the home is owned by the person not making their house payments. They aren't going to just open the door for you to walk through and check everything out. This means that you are buying a home without knowing its true condition. What if the person living in the home was a little upset with the foreclosing lender? Do you think that they might be a little hard on the house? What if they stole the furnace? Or what if they clogged the drains and turned the water on?

In my opinion, it is too risky to buy real estate at the sheriff's sale. Now, I know some investors are very successful at it. But for the average part-time investor, there are better strategies with reduced risk.

I will share one funny story with you. An investor friend of mine likes to buy properties at sheriff sales. And one day she was at a sale bidding on a particular home. (When you bid at a sheriff sale, you are required to have a cashier's check for 10% of the purchase price for the down payment.) Because she had researched this particular home, she was prepared for the bid with her 10% cashier's check. She lost out on the bid for the home she had researched, but had heard about some vacant land close by that was being auctioned off. Knowing the area and the price of lots, she figured that the land was worth about $15,000. Nobody else was bidding, so she put in a bid and it was accepted.

After paying for the lot, she found out that it was submerged under water. We live near Lake Erie. Her lot was actually in the Lake. No wonder it was such a good deal!

What I Learned…

I finally learned the dollar per hour earned trying to buy sheriff sale homes isn't worth the risk. You see, there are so many risky factors that can steal your profit when you try to buy beat up homes. To name just a few:

1. Your repair costs could be higher then you estimated. An estimated $500 repair job could turn into a $4,000 repair job. Whoops, there goes $3,500 of profit!!

2. It could take you an extra six months to sell the home. An extra six months of paying the utilities, property taxes and mortgage payment. That could easily eat up another $5,000 of profit. We have a client that purchased a fixer-upper home a year ago and it is still for sale to this day. Every month, she has to cover the costs of this home without any income coming in.

3. You aren't able to resell the home at the price you estimated when you purchased the property.

4. You are lucky enough to sell your home, but your buyer's loan gets rejected at the last minute, which means you are back to the beginning...

The reality is that if you are a beginning investor doing this in your spare time, the odds are against you. If you are going to take time away from your family to invest in real estate, you should be compensated accordingly. Who in their right mind would take a second part-time job and actually have to pay their employer? If you try to buy, fix up and flip homes, you very well could lose money. My guess is that there is a strong chance that you will lose money.

Is there a better way?????

Now for a strictly Canadian perspective...

Throughout this book we'll be sharing how we now suggest you go about investing, however, to give some context to our recommendations let's briefly go back in time.

Growing up, my father dabbled in real estate by flipping a couple of houses and renting out a large 4000 sq. foot home in an upscale area of Mississauga, Ontario. He made tens of thousands of dollars on his first flip but got hit with the huge real estate collapse of the early 1990s on his second attempt. His purchase of $700,000+ lost hundreds of thousands of dollars in value months after the purchase and the house had not even been built yet.

Years later, I began absorbing all the real estate investing information available to me. I spent thousands on books, tapes (yes, tapes!), CDs and weekend courses by U.S. based investors trying to teach Canadians how to invest.

I learned the hard way that you can waste a lot of time doing the wrong things. After reading all the books, it seemed obvious that the way to make money was to write up offers asking for the seller to take a Vendor Take Back mortgage. Well, as mentioned earlier, over the last 10 years interest rates have been so low that this approach did not work. This had more appeal back in the 1980s when interest rates were much higher and sellers had to accept creative strategies if they wanted to sell their home.

My wasted time included searching for homes without the help of an agent, making private offers using agreements that I had drafted myself, then having to explain the Vendor Take Back clauses in the agreements to the seller, then being told where to go!

Not a fun time!

Sheriff auctions work slightly differently in Canada so all the U.S. based material I was reading really didn't apply to my situation. Nevertheless, I began going to the Toronto property auctions and combing the Ontario Gazette for properties being sold under distress. We quickly found that the competition here was so intense that the opportunity to find a money making deal would require months of time investment.

We then found limited Canadian investing information but it all came from people who spoke about investing but would never actually go hit the streets with you. They would preach what to do but you could never get them to actually go make offers with you in the real world. The most you could get would be a monthly email or meeting of some sort. We wanted answers, not emails!

When looking for properties we found it difficult to get anyone to answer things like:

Where is the best place to advertise a rental property?

How fast can we expect to rent it out?

How do we limit the number of tenant phone calls we receive on the property?

How do we create auction like environments for renting out the homes quickly?

How much can we expect in rent?

What rate are homes in area appreciating at?

What is the typical rent in the area?

What do people in this area look for when buying or renting a house?

Both of us then decided we would buy and flip houses and we both had different and very interesting experiences. We both made money, but it was more like we had created jobs for ourselves. Real Estate 'investing' is about creating 'cash flow', not work!

18

3

A Simple SLOW Wealth-Building Strategy

Adding income and building your wealth with real estate is simple, but it is not easy. In this chapter, I will show you just how simply you can create a wealth-building machine. To get started, let's compare the strategy of buying sheriff sale homes, fixing them up and then selling them to the Buy and Hold strategy. When I say Buy and Hold, I mean investing in a single-family home and renting it out to a tenant. You just keep renting this one home out to tenants each and every year. Your tenant pays you enough rent to cover your mortgage payment, property taxes and insurance. You probably won't be making a lot of money each month with this strategy in the beginning, but the long-term wealth building opportunity is incredible. Each year, you will be able to raise your rents a little. Over time, your cash flow will increase while your monthly payment stays the same.

To keep the numbers simple and very conservative, let's assume you buy a nice $200,000 home. This home has three bedrooms and one bathroom. To invest in this home, you go to the bank and get a typical investor loan requiring you to have a 10% down payment. (Our team's investing clients have access to a special 5% down payment investor loan program. More on this later in the book.) Let's review the numbers on this investment:

Purchase Price	$200,000	
Down Payment	$20,000	(10% Down Investor Loan)
Mortgage Loan	$180,000	(Fixed 4.5% Rate, 30 Year Loan)
Monthly Loan Payment (rounded)	$900	
Monthly Property Taxes	$175	
Monthly Insurance	$50	
Monthly PMI	$75	(Private Mortgage Insurance)
Total Monthly Payment	$1200	
Monthly Rental Income	$1300	
Monthly Positive Cash Flow	$100	

Based on the example above, you as the investor would be earning $100 each and every month from this single-family home. That doesn't sound like a great deal of money, does it? It doesn't really seem like it's worth all of the hassle. Invest $20,000 and get $100 each month….

If that were all that you earned, it probably wouldn't be a great deal. However, this one home really is a wealth-building machine. This one home would provide you with four income streams. By investing in one single-family home, you would be adding the financial security of four income streams.

Here are your four income streams:

1. **Monthly Positive Cash flow** – In the example above, you would be earning an extra $100 each month from this investment. You can take the $100 and go out to a dinner and a movie. Well OK, maybe just a movie.

2. **Mortgage Loan Reduction** - I also call this Equity Build Up. What I mean is that each month the tenant pays the rent; you send a mortgage payment to your lender. A portion of your mortgage payment is reducing the loan balance. Every dollar in loan that is paid down is wealth to you. In fact, your tenant is paying off your debts. Not too bad. In this example, about $250 dollars of your payment reduces your outstanding loan. This in another income stream to you each month.

3. **Appreciation** – Each year you own this rental property, its value will be increasing. If your $200,000 home appreciates at 4% a year, your home would be worth $208,000 after the first year you owned it. That $10,000 increase is another income stream. If I divide this $10,000 increase by 12 months, it would amount to $667 each month.

4. **Tax Savings** – At the end of the year, your rental property will show a loss on paper for tax purposes. The reason is that the IRS and CRA allow you to include an expense called depreciation on your tax return. You don't have to pay for this expense. This extra expense creates a tax loss, which you can use to reduce the amount of taxes you pay for the year. Let's assume that

this loss saves you $1,000 in taxes. $1,000 divided by 12 months is $83 dollars each month.

One single-family rental home at the example cost of $200,000 provides you with these four income streams. If I added up these four income streams, they would total the following:

Monthly Positive Cash flow	$100
Monthly Loan Reduction	$250
Monthly Price Appreciation	$667
Monthly Tax Savings	$83
Total Monthly Return	$1,100

Not bad if you ask me. But really this is just a simple example showing a house at the cost of $200,000. What happens when you have a house at $250,000, $300,000 or more? You guessed it; your returns are much, much higher!

But what is the real reason real estate is such an incredible wealth-building machine?

The Majority of this Monthly Profit is Locked Up

Of the $1,100 in Monthly Return in our simple example, you can only mess up by spending $100 dollars each month. The rest is locked up, so to speak. It is very difficult to spend your monthly loan reduction, or your monthly price appreciation. Each month, you are getting richer by $1,100. This $1,100 monthly income occurs without you saving any money out of your paycheck or investing in your retirement plan.

If you had a different investment that paid you the $1,100 in cash, you might be tempted to use that money to buy "Toys." (Toys are TVs, computers, and vacations.) Getting wealthy and creating extra income is very hard if you are spending all of your profits. You don't have to fight the urge to spend your income because you can't get at it. If you are having a bad month, you are unable to withdraw cash from your house, which protects your income!

In my opinion, having your monthly profits locked up is what makes real estate incredibly powerful. All a person has to do is buy one home and rent it to a tenant. Well, I guess you would have to make sure that the tenant paid their rent and that you paid your monthly mortgage payment, taxes and insurance, too. This one investment would provide you with an invisible $1,100 monthly wealth-building machine.

I can probably hear you challenging me on this:

1. What happens if I can't get my home rented out?

My guess is that the rent you are asking is too high. A mistake that most investors make is to wait too long to reduce the asking price for the monthly rent. If it takes you two or three months to rent your home, you could be losing $2,400 to $3,600. If you just dropped your rent by $50, you would possibly rent your home faster, putting more income in your pocket for the year. By dropping your rent by $25, you are only losing $600. Don't hesitate drop the rent and get your home rented as fast as possible. Later in the book, I will show you how to prevent this from happening before you even buy a property!

2. What happens if I my tenants don't pay their monthly rent?

You might have to evict them. I have been renting properties for 11 years now. For my first 10 years, I never had to evict one tenant. In 2004, I had to evict two tenants. A third one paid his back rent on the day of the court hearing. Considering the big picture, this doesn't happen all that much. I realize that evicting a tenant sounds ugly and scary, but it really is a simple court matter that takes about five minutes of your time.

The rules for eviction vary from state to state and city to city, so check with your area for the specifics. In my area, if your tenants don't pay their rent, you mail them a special three day notice in the regular and certified mail with receipt. You also need to deliver or post a notice on the actual residence. If they don't respond to this special three day notice, you fax your lease and a copy of the three day notice you sent to your tenant to your attorney. He files the paperwork with the appropriate court. You show up at court on the date assigned. The hearing takes five minutes max. If you have to speak to the judge, you simply tell the judge when the tenant stopped paying their rent. The judge issues the order and it's over. In my area the whole process takes about 30 days, so you would lose one month's rent in the process. To protect you, get a double security deposit, or collect the last month's rent up front.

The funny part about evictions is that many people won't invest in real estate because they are scared of having to evict a tenant. This one fear holds them back from a $1,100 monthly wealth-building machine. In the example above, if the tenant hadn't paid their rent, I would have had to make the mortgage payment of $1,200 out of my pocket. Yes, that would stink. I have done it before and I am not really excited about it.

However, if I can get you to look at it differently, it may change your perspective dramatically. You would be paying $1,200 to cover the monthly total payment. However, your profit on that $1,200 would be $1,100. (This was determined by taking the total monthly profit above $1,100 and subtracting out the $100 of positive cash flow because you didn't receive it.) This is a 91% return on your investment. ($1100 return / $1200 investment.) Instead, many people invest their money in a mutual fund that earns an 8% to 10% return on investment.

The way to look at having to make a rental property mortgage payment is that you are investing your money at a 70% rate of return. In the big picture, how are you losing? Most people look at making a monthly payment on their properties as a loss. I would recommend that you shift your thinking and view the payment as an investment with a very high rate of return.

If this is still a big concern for you, you can rent your home out to tenants who are on a government program. These tenants receive benefits from public authorities who pay their rent. Depending on the tenant's situation, the program either will pay for their entire rent payment, or a portion of it. I have two properties with tenants such as these. Each month, I receive a check on the first of the month directly from the government. I don't have to chase the rent or worry if the check will bounce.

For the Buy and Hold strategy, you can consider this strategy for tenants because your monthly rent is guaranteed. Whoops, did I just say guaranteed? Let me change that to: your monthly rent will continue to come to you until the specific government program ends. Remember, there are no guarantees. I wouldn't recommend having all of your properties on such programs because relying on ONE source for payment is too risky.

3. What about maintenance and repairs to the home?

Yes, you will have to make repairs to the home. However, if you buy the right property, you can dramatically minimize the repairs you will have to make. For the most part, the money you need to invest in the home is to paint and carpet the property. When a tenant moves out, you might need to re-paint a few rooms, or replace the carpeting. When looking for a rental property to invest in, look for a home with newer windows, newer roof, newer furnace and air conditioning. These are the items that could cost you a lot of money if you have to replace them. We teach our clients to look for homes that have had many updates to minimize costly repairs.

OK, let's just continue on with this example. Assume that you purchase this one rental property for $200,000. Over the years, you kept the home rented out and continued to make your mortgage payment. Each year, you sent a letter to your tenant increasing the rent by $15 a month. A $15 rent increase each year isn't a big increase. Your tenants won't move out on you. Plus, if you do it consistently each year, they will begin to expect and plan for it. You follow this SIMPLE plan each year for 30 years.

At the end of 30 years, your one rental property would be worth $662,699. The monthly rental income you would be receiving would be approximately $1,650. After year 30, your 30-year mortgage would be paid in full and you would be pocketing the entire $1,650 each and every month.

Big Picture Thinking: You invested $20,000 30 years ago and now have an asset fully paid for valued at $662,699 (est. 4% avg. annual appreciation) that pays you $1,650 each and every month whether you're sick, vacationing or fishing. Can it get any better than this? I don't understand why more people don't buy just one rental property and hold it for life. If you followed this simple approach with 3 homes, you would have assets worth $1,988,097 and a monthly income of $4,950.

And, again, I have to mention that this is just a simple example with one home at $200,000. What if you had several homes and/or the home costs were $250,000 or $300,000 dollars. The wealth building could be practically infinite!

By having three rental properties, you would have added 12 additional monthly income streams, which is much better than ONE stream from your job. Three homes would provide a $4,950 monthly wealth-building machine for you and your family.

If this sounds good to you, just wait until you read about using the Rent-to-Own strategy. It takes the Buy and Hold approach to a new level.

Now for a strictly Canadian perspective...

With all the knowledge shared around the power of real estate investment and the great wealth it has created it is hard to understand why more people haven't purchased at least one investment property.

You could take almost any person with a high net worth and see a real estate holding in their investment portfolio somewhere. No matter what industry they generated their wealth or what age they are now, they see it as a viable investment.

What gets me is why it is seen as such a risk to so many people. An average person works hard for their money and, in Canada, pays a good piece of it to taxes. We then take the money we have earned, after tax of course, and want to invest it to make more money. It seems simple so far.

Here is the mystery: most people will go into the bank and ask a 'personal banker' where they should invest their money. They have no background information on this person and no idea the level of wealth they have accumulated. However, most decide to trust their banker with their money and hope they can make something of it.

One of the most outrageous things I have ever heard around this has to do with a friend of mine. For a number of years in her twenties she was employed by one of the 'Big Five' banks in Canada. She was a 'Personal Banker' the title may have changed but essentially she had one of the little offices at the side of the bank branch.

People would make appointments to visit with her to discuss their financial situation and she would offer guidance and insight into different investment vehicles that were available to them. She would even make recommendations on what to do with their hard earned wealth. What they didn't know was that this girl was in a very poor financial situation herself, had never invested before, and had no successful track record of helping other people. Yet she was considered worthy enough to guide other equally as knowledgeable people into investing.

I don't want to focus on the banking industry but I think it is important to take this story and associate it with 'risk'.

In my early investing days, people constantly told me that what I was doing was very risky. Well you know what? In part, they were right.

There is some risk involved with investing in real estate but no more than most other investment vehicles. I actually think there is less, a lot less.

When you invest in real estate you own a tangible asset. It is something that you can see and control. You can make improvements to it if necessary to increase its value. Similar to what we spoke of with a small rent change, You can make minor changes to ensure a good return is still attainable.

The key is you have **control over your investmen**t.

Instead, you hand your money over to a stranger at the bank and hoping that they invest it wisely for you. Then, you hope the vehicle they chose appreciates. Then, you hope that it stays that way so you don't lose your gains or your initial investment.

You can see there is a lot of finger crossing in that scenario. Maybc you like the security a GIC holds. But with our historically low interest rates, do you realize that many pay about 1.5% over inflation? At that rate, how long will it take you to achieve your financial goals?

We are going to share with you an extremely powerful way to invest that will give you greater control over your investment in real estate than many other approaches. In the book '*Why We Want You to be Rich*' by Robert Kiyosaki and Donald Trump, they explain that the real meaning of risk is little or no control.

When you hand your money over to someone else you no longer have control, you only have hope.

It is time to take little baby steps outside of your comfort zone so that it expands and you grow as a person. As you continue to grow as a person, what you had previously seen as a limit starts to diminish and you realize that the only limits are the ones you have placed on yourself.

I just can't figure out why not everybody would invest in at least one single rental property over the course of their life. Did you see the numbers earlier in this chapter? You might want to go back and take a look at them and see if that type of return on your investment can fit into your portfolio somewhere.

The long term return on your money will be great. The long term return on your personal growth cannot be measured.

4

How $10,000 Can Make You Wealthy! The Buy and Hold Strategy Kicked Up a Notch...

You gotta love Emeril! During my early years of investing in real estate, I started testing other strategies. Well, to make a long story short, I purchased a few multi-family properties and then quickly resold them because of the intense management required. I then purchased commercial property and resold it because of the difficulty in securing new tenants when you have a vacancy. What I finally settled on, with great success, is a whole new way to profit from real estate. This approach combined the best parts of the Flipping Homes strategy and the best parts of the Buy and Hold strategy. In the examples below, I summarize the best parts of both investing approaches.

Flipping Homes Strategy

1. Cashing Out--Selling your property to a buyer and receiving a large profit

2. No Management–Not having to be a landlord

Buy and Hold Strategy

1. Monthly Cash flow – Receiving income each month from your investment

31

2. Tax Benefits – Saving money on your taxes because of a tax loss each year

3. Appreciation – Profiting from the annual increase in the property value

4. Equity Increase – Each month the tenant pays your loan balance down

When you are an investor, you typically want the best of both worlds. You want large paychecks with long-term wealth. When you flip homes, you aren't building long-term wealth. You are in essence creating a job for yourself. What I mean is that when you flip a home, you get paid. To get paid again, you have to go out and flip another home. For me, I don't want another job. I would rather work one time and get paid over and over again! I want wealth without working. My guess is that you don't want another job, either.

Well, I stumbled across an idea that combined the best of both investing approaches.

The Flip & Buy and Hold Blend!!!!!

I finally figured out a way to:

1. Put my real estate investing on auto-pilot (not have to play landlord every day)

2. Receive a high monthly cash flow

3. Maintain the annual tax loss and qualify for the ability to sell homes without paying taxes at the time of the sale

32

4. Cash Out--receive a substantial profit check within a few short years

5. Lock in two years of appreciation

6. Lock in two years of equity increase

7. Get a large check (3% of the value) from my property within a few short weeks of my purchase and ownership

What I have learned to do is blend renting single-family homes using the Buy and Hold approach with flipping single-family homes. I know this might sound a little confusing, but let me explain how this works.

I buy a nice single-family home in a nice area. I then sell this home under a short-term Rent to Own program to a tenant/buyer.

What in the Heck is Rent-to-Own?

It's actually not that complicated at all. You simply buy a nice single-family home and rent it to a tenant who wants to own his or her own home. You have your tenant sign a lease agreement for one, two or three years. During this time, you have a lease agreement with the tenant. In addition, you have a separate agreement that provides your tenant the option to buy your home at any point during the lease term for a pre-agreed selling price. The tenant has the option to buy the home, not the obligation. If they buy the home, they have to purchase at the agreed upon price. If they don't purchase at the end of their lease, you can continue renting to them or terminate the lease agreement. If you decide to terminate the lease agreement, you can offer your nice single-family home to a new tenant on a new Rent-to-Own program. Understand that there are many ways to structure the lease and option agreement that will substantially increase the odds that your tenant will buy the home outright during their tenancy. One of the best ways to increase your odds is to offer to credit a portion of their monthly rent payment toward their down payment if they should buy the home. So, in essence, during the lease term, your tenants are automatically saving money for the down payment.

The big picture with this approach is that you are not trying to outright flip homes. You don't have the risk of repair costs exceeding budget because you are not buying a fixer upper home. You are buying nice homes in nice areas. You don't have expensive carrying costs waiting for the home to sell, because you have a tenant paying you each month until they buy it. You don't have to make manual repairs yourself or have to oversee subcontractors repairing your properties. You still get the big payoff when the tenant buys the home, just as you would if you had flipped the home.

My goal is to buy a home 10% below value and then sell it to the tenant when the home appreciates by 10%.

In my area, homes are appreciating at about 5% per year. So if I offer a two-year rent to own, the value of the home at the end of the second year is 10% more than it is today. So, I profit 20% within two years. On a $100,000 home, this amounts to $20,000. In some areas, homes are appreciating at a rate that is much more than 5%. In these areas, the profits would be much greater than 20% within the first two years.

Here is an actual investment that I just completed, to show you how this works. You can see many real life examples later in the book. I purchased a nice three-bedroom, two-bath colonial on a tree lined street very close to where I live in Willoughby, Ohio. For this home, I paid $116,500. To buy this home, I obtained a loan from a bank that required a 10% down payment. (Our Income for Life Members now have access to 5% down investor loan programs.) My total monthly payment on the home with taxes and insurance is about $925. As soon as title transferred into my name, I put out a sign in the front yard stating, "Rent-to-Own." These words have become my favorite three words because they are so profitable. I had a person call from the sign who wanted to see the home. I showed him the home and he completed a rental application. I checked his credit and verified his references and decided to rent to him. I rented the home to him on a two-year Rent to Own program (two-year lease with the option to buy anytime during the two years) under the following terms:

1. He paid an up-front payment of $4,500

2. His monthly rent is $1,245

3. At the end of two years, his buyout price is $140,000.

4. Every month that he makes his rent payment on time, he will receive a credit toward the down payment of $300. (Understand that this monthly credit comes off of the sale price if he buys the home. If he doesn't buy the home, all monies paid are considered rent and are not refundable.)

How about these numbers!!!!!!

I invested a down payment, $11,650 on this home. I received a check from my tenant/buyer in the amount of $4,500 UP FRONT within two weeks from my taking ownership. I also profit $320 every month ($1,245 received in rent and my monthly payment is $925). At the end of one year, my monthly profit, or positive cash flow is $3,840 plus the up-front amount of $4,500, for a total return of $8,340. By dividing $8,340 (profit in year one) by $11,650 (total amount invested), the return on investment is 71.58%.

In year two, I will still profit by $320 per month, plus the profit at the time of the sale between my purchase price and my resale price. If the tenant buys out the home, his purchase price is $140,000 less his up-front payment of $4,500, less the earned monthly credit of $7,200 ($300 per month for 24 months). This comes out to $128,300 to me less my purchase price of $116,500 leaves a sale price profit of $11,800. Plus at the time of sale to my tenant, I get my down payment of $11,650 back. The check I receive at closing is $23,450. I doubled my original investment in two years if my tenant buys the home from me.

In summary, my investment pays me $4,500 up front, $325 a month for two years and $11,800 at the end of two years, for a grand total of $24,100 plus my original down payment of $11,650 back. This amounts to a 206% return on my investment. Had I used a 5% down loan program, my return on investment would have been a whopping 413%. My guess is that this beats the stock market!

OK, I know you're thinking, what happens if the tenant doesn't buy the home?

It's actually more profitable for me if he doesn't. If he doesn't buy the home, his up-front payment is not refundable, nor is any portion of his monthly rent. So at the end of the two-year lease, I would start a new Rent to Own with someone else and earn a new up-front payment with higher monthly rents. If the tenant never buys the home out, I still continue to receive all of the benefits of the Buy and Hold strategy. It is like a super-charged rental property.

Understand that I don't want this to happen. I really want the tenant to buy the home. My guess is that because of the way that this program is structured, he will buy the home. At the end of two years, he will have a total of $11,700 toward the down payment. With such a large amount, he won't walk away from the home.

So it truly becomes win/ win for everyone.

Investors that use this approach literally create five income streams from one single-family home. See the picture on the next page of the five income streams created from a single Rent-to-Own program:

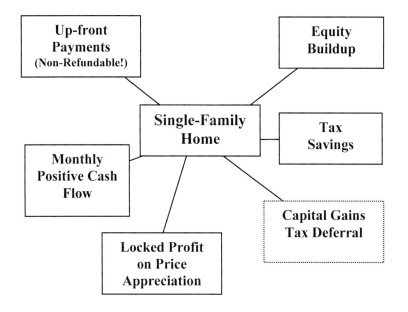

From the picture above, you can see how you have five income streams from just one home. Four of these income streams have been explained previously in this book. The one income stream that wasn't explained is the up-front payment. This is a very lucrative stream. In most cases, this stream is three to five percent of the value of the home. Many investors don't realize that they can receive this kind of income from their properties. If you invested in three homes this year and received $4,000 up front on those properties, you would have an extra $12,000 in your pocket, which isn't a bad part-time income all by itself!

I understand that you are skeptical about this. You are asking yourself, how do investors get tenants to give them such a big up-front non-refundable payment? To understand why this happens, you need to put yourself in the proper perspective. First, understand that most people want to own their own home. In fact, in a recent survey performed by the National Association of Realtors, the number one reason a renter bought a home was "To Own Their Own Home." It is an American dream to own a home. The problem is that a buyer needs one of two things to make this happen. They need either money or good credit. If the person has both, that is fantastic. If they have money and bad credit, they still might be able to buy a home. Most lenders will provide loans to buyers with poor credit if they have a down payment of 20%. On a $120,000 home, the buyer with poor credit would need $24,000 down to buy a home today. However, if the person has good credit they can easily find loans available with no down payment.

The opportunity comes from the segment of buyers that don't fit either of these two categories. The category I am referring to is the buyer that has some money and has poor credit. A buyer in this scenario doesn't have the ability to buy a home today because they don't have 20% down. Understand that they still have a strong desire to own a home; they just don't have a way to make it happen with the mortgage lenders. This is the category of buyers that you can attract when you offer a Rent-to-Own program on your home.

The Rent-to-Own program offers people with some money and poor credit a chance to move in to their own home today without having to qualify for a mortgage loan. During the lease period, they can work to improve their credit score by paying their bills on time. By improving their credit score and earning additional credits toward the down payment, they can improve their chances of qualifying for a mortgage. Most of our clients use 12-month, 18-month or 24-month Rent-to-Own programs. In each case, the tenant would have that much time to aggressively work to improve their credit score.

What it really boils down to is an underlying philosophy of:

LANDLORD WIN / TENANT WIN

As Zig Ziglar always says, *"You can have everything you want in life, if you just help enough other people get what they want."* This approach works because the tenant has something at stake. The tenant has to have something on the table to lose. They must have something to look for at the end of the rainbow. You are probably thinking that this is easier said than done. Not so. I know this will be a shift in your old way of thinking based on the old investing techniques. The Rent-to-Own program is based on Win/Win. Our client members rent their homes with every intention of helping the tenant buy the home at the end of the lease. The majority of our clients…

Don't Want to Be a Landlord… And Quite Frankly, Neither Do I

The best part of a Rent-to-Own program is that you are not a landlord. I tell my tenants that legally I own the home during the lease period, but for all intents and purposes, I consider it their home. My lease states that they can't make major alterations to the home without my approval, but I want them to make the home as nice as possible. I want them to paint the deck and add new landscaping. The more they invest into the home, the better the chances of them buying out at the end.

Here are some quick tidbits about the agreement my rent-to-own tenants sign. *(We provide our Income for Life Members with all of these legal documents for their own use.)*

1. The tenant is responsible for the first $200 of repairs in each month. I am responsible for the balance. Since I buy nicer homes, there typically aren't any major repairs. Yes, there are always minor repairs like clogged drains and leaky plumbing, but the tenant pays the first $200, which in most cases covers the whole thing.

2. The tenant is only eligible for the $300 monthly credit toward the down payment if they pay their rent on or before the first of the month. So now they have a huge incentive to pay me on time.

3. The lease agreement states that the tenant is responsible for mowing the lawn, trimming the shrubs and shoveling the driveway.

These three and a few other clauses in our rent-to-own contracts place the management of the property in the tenant's hands. They understand right from the beginning that they are responsible for the home. In many cases, our tenants make repairs to the properties without even telling us about them. Your tenants will operate the same way if you teach them right from the beginning how you operate. It also helps to have the right contracts to make sure that everyone understands their responsibilities.

Two other incredible benefits you would receive by using the Rent-to-Own investing approach are the ability to avoid paying Realtor commissions and deferring the capital gains tax on the sales proceeds.

Realtor Commissions: If you had planned to sell your home the typical way, you would more than likely have to hire a Realtor to help you. My guess is that the average real estate commission is 6%. On a $100,000 home, you would pay $6,000 at closing to the real estate agent. The reason why you would need a Realtor is to help you find a qualified buyer to purchase your home at your price. With the Rent-to-Own system, you already have the buyer living in your home. They have also already agreed to buy your home at your price. This price was agreed upon in writing before they even moved into the home. This simply means that you do not need to hire a Realtor, which saves you $6,000 or more to sell your home!

Deferring Your Capital Gains Tax: Selling an asset that you hold for investment usually triggers a capital gain for tax purposes. This gain is taxed at various income tax rates. If you invested in 1,000 shares of Microsoft stock 10 years ago for $40 per share and sold that stock today for $80 per share, you would have a gain of $40 per share or $40,000. If you were taxed at 15%, you would owe $6,000 in capital gains taxes. However, the game is different with real estate investing. There is a section in the IRS code that allows you to reinvest all of your proceeds on the sale of rental real estate into similar properties and not pay any tax at the time of the sale. This is known as a 1031 tax-free exchange. This special section in the IRS code allows you to take ALL of your profits from the sale of your home to your tenant and use them to buy more rental real estate.

Although in Canada the 1031 exchange is not available, as much as half of your capital gains are tax free. This means you are taxed at a much lower rate than regular income and it can allow you to benefit is a similar way. These provisions in the tax code bring me to my next strategy:

When You Sell Your Home to Your Tenant
Trade One Home for <u>Two or Three</u> Homes...

To invest in real estate you need to have a down payment. The typical investor buys properties with a 10% down payment. (Our client members use a special 5% down payment investor loan program. If you would like access to this same loan program, consider giving our Income for Life Membership a try. With your membership, you get access to all of our preferred programs. See inside this book for a special trial offer.)

You can use this one down payment to buy three homes. Many investors have to have three separate down payments to buy three separate homes.

You can use one down payment to buy three homes by selling your first home to your tenant and re-investing in two more single-family homes. You will use the proceeds from the sale of the home as down payments on multiple properties.

You can continue to repeat the process. You can repeat the process over and over again. You only need to start with one house.

That's some serious leverage in action.

By applying this strategy over and over, you can build a real empire of real estate.

Here is a picture of what I mean:

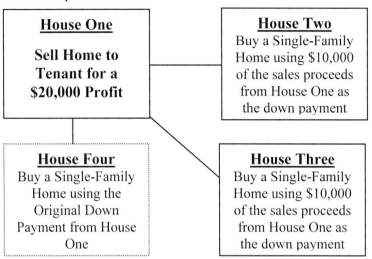

From the sale of house one, you would also be receiving your original down payment back. You could use this down payment to buy House Four! You can trade one home for three homes. This is massive leverage. Remember from above that one Rent-to-Own investment property provides you with five income streams. Three homes would therefore provide you with 15 automatic income streams (five income streams per home). The challenge we all face is to continuously create multiple income streams. If we have multiple income streams, we don't have to be as dependent upon just one stream–like your job!

The sad truth is that the majority of people go through life with only one income stream. They work hard to get a good job, and then they stop working for more income streams. I feel that you have an obligation each month to be working to create additional income streams. For me, this book represents a new income stream. I own a real estate brokerage. Within this company, there are several separate income streams. Outside of this company, I receive 22 checks each month from my tenants. If you have 22 properties and each property has five income streams within it, how many automatic wealth-building streams are working in your favor? The number of monthly rent checks that I receive continues to grow each year as I invest in more properties. I probably have over 30 income streams right now and I am writing a book to add another stream. I also have several ideas that I am working on for new income streams. Please understand that I am not including this to brag. I only include this to show you that building income streams is and should be your full-time focus. Don't just settle for one income stream from your job. It is far too risky. Here is an idea you can use to quickly and easily add additional income streams into your life…

House One: Offer this home on a one-year Rent-to-Own program. If you structure your program properly, you can increase the odds of your tenant buying the home at the end of the year. We help our clients structure their Rent-to-Own programs to increase the odds that their tenant will buy it at the end of the lease. In addition, in our Income for Life Newsletter, we teach our members other creative ways to sell homes to their tenants if they still don't qualify for a mortgage loan! Back to House One: You would receive an up-front payment of a few thousand dollars plus a positive monthly cash flow and a big payoff at the end of year one. ***The goal of the payoff amount should be enough profit to use as a down payment on two or more additional single-family homes. (Remember you will get your original down payment back when you sell the home..***

As you could probably see, this could snowball into a large group of homes. My goal is not to live off of the profits from the sale of the homes, but to create the monthly positive cash flow from these homes to cover all of my living expenses. I figured that if my monthly living expenses were covered by the cash flow from my real estate investments, I would be financially free! In order to accomplish this goal, I needed to continuously re-invest the sale profits into more homes to increase my monthly cash flow. If you were to sell a rental home and not reinvest the proceeds, your money machine would be gone. It would be like shooting the goose that lays the golden eggs. Don't make this mistake! You will regret it, I promise.

THE TRUE DEFINITION OF WEALTH

If you have ever read any of Robert Kiyosaki's books ("Rich Dad Poor Dad Series"), he says that you shouldn't measure your wealth in terms of money in the bank or material possessions you own; rather, you should measure wealth in terms of time. To determine if you are wealthy, you have to ask yourself one question:

How Long Can You Live Financially Without Having to Physically Work for Money?

To help clarify this thought further, let me give you an example: Let's say that you have $2,000 a month of expenses for mortgage, car, debts, food and everything else. If you had $1,000 a month of income or cash flow from your rent-to-own homes, you could conceivably live two out of every four weeks without having to go physically work for money. So in this example, if you could increase your monthly cash flow from your real estate investments by $1,000 to meet your current standard of living at $2,000 per month, you would be wealthy. You would be free to choose how you want to spend your time rather than be forced to go to work every day. Now, this concept doesn't mean that you should live in a shack and drive a green Pinto; it simply means that you should create enough cash flow from your Rent-to-Own homes to meet whatever standard of living you would like to have.

Let's take a moment and think about life on a big scale. Can you find a way to come up with funds to buy just one rental property in the next 12 months? If you had access to our special 5% down investor loan program, this wouldn't be that difficult. If you can just get started, you can literally build an investing machine that grows by itself. The trick is to get started—to do whatever it takes to get one single-family investment home. Here is just one simple example of how one home snowballs for you:

Invest in one $120,000 Home. With our special 5% down payment loan program, you would need $6,000 down. We would negotiate to have your loan closing costs paid by the seller. Offer this home on a Rent-to-Own program and go for a $5,000 up-front payment. Use the $5,000 upfront payment you receive from your tenant/buyer as a down payment on your second home. Follow this same process and buy three single-family homes in 12 months. This approach would allow you to buy three single-family investment homes for under $10,000 out of your pocket. If you received cash flow of $300 from each home, you would be generating an extra $900 of income each month. For my family, this was enough to allow my wife to quit her job! However, if you could follow this approach and acquire three homes in the next 12 months, you could have complete financial freedom in just seven years.

I'd also like to point out that this example works just as well, if not better, with a house that's purchased for $200,000 or $300,000. These homes will require a little more cash up front, but they will also earn more down payment money because of their higher value. That down payment money can easily be put toward the next property, allowing the snowball to roll free. The rest is history.

If you were to invest in three homes in the next 12 months and offer these homes on two-year rent-to-own programs, you could create a real estate empire that would last for years. When your tenants in these three homes buy the homes, you invest the proceeds into two additional homes. You should have enough money from the proceeds of each sale to use for down payments on two new properties. Continue the Rent-to-Own program on each new property that you invest in. On each sale, use a 1031 tax-free exchange to defer any taxes due. If you were to follow this simple approach, you would be amazed at how quickly things would happen:

The Numbers are Staggering

By the End of Your Seventh Year –

<u>YOU WILL OWN 24 HOMES</u>

If you average $150 in monthly cash flow per home-
Your Total Monthly Cash flow is $3,600 - **$43,200 per year**

If you average $200 in monthly cash flow per home-
Your Total Monthly Cash flow is $4,800 - **$57,600 per year**

If you average $250 in monthly cash flow per home-
Your Total Monthly Cash flow is $6,000 - **$72,000 per year**

If you average $300 in monthly cash flow per home-
Your Total Monthly Cash flow is $7,200 - **$86,400 per year**

Remember, earlier I showed you how to get started by investing in three homes for a minimal amount out of your pocket. You were able to do this by having your houses buy more houses. Would you have believed that this small investment could create an annual income of $86,400 in just seven years? This investment amount is much less than the cost of a new car.

Your financial future and wealth are dependent on you getting a small up-front amount of money and buying three single-family homes in the next 12 months. Can you do it? I know you can do it, I just hope you will do it.

Common Questions on The Rent-to-Own Program

1. *What happens if the tenant doesn't buy the home at the end of their lease?*
   In most cases, the tenants are earning a large monthly credit toward the purchase of the property. In addition, they have given a large non-refundable up-front payment at the beginning of the lease. Because they literally have thousands of dollars on the line, they will do everything they can to buy the home. But if they don't buy the home, the agreement stipulates that all monies paid will be considered rent, and the credits will be non-refundable. After the tenant moves out of the home, I start a new Rent-to-Own program at inflation-adjusted numbers *(which increases my overall return on investment)*.

2. *Do the tenant/buyers understand that they could lose a lot of money if they don't buy the home?*
   Yes, this is explained and stated in writing in the very beginning. We explain to the prospective tenant that they must be 100% committed to buying this home before the end of the lease. We tell them that if they aren't 100% committed to buying the home, they shouldn't get involved with our program because they will not receive any of their

money back. We also explain that the up-front money they pay is not refundable because we are taking our home off the market and we our investing into a two-year partnership to help them own their own home. The money paid would be compensation to us for the loss of two years.

3. ***Do you want them to buy the home?***
Yes. I truly want to help someone that might not have ever owned a home actually become a homeowner. Remember Zig Ziglar's saying, **"You can have everything you want in life if you just help enough other people get what they want."**

4. ***Do I have to save the monthly credits that the tenant is earning in a separate bank account?***
Not if you use our agreements! You will never have to write a check to your tenant for the monthly credits that they earn. If they buy your home, the credits earned will be subtracted off of their purchase price at the Title Company. You will receive your sales price less the monthly credits earned. If the tenant doesn't buy your home, all the money is considered rent and is not refundable.

5. ***What if I don't want to sell my investment property?***
My suggestion would be for you to not get attached to a particular property. One of my clients views his single-family homes as "little cash boxes." To him, the house itself doesn't matter. The income paid to him from the house matters. You should focus on getting attached to a profitable investing approach, not a home. Your role as a real estate investor is to extract as much cash as possible from as many properties as possible. ***Don't get attached to the property. Get attached to the system.***

6. *What rent do you charge?*
I tend to charge 10-20% over what the fair market value monthly rent would be. My goal is to try to have a monthly positive cash flow of $200 from each property. Sometimes it is less and sometimes it is more. The program can even work without positive cash flow in areas of higher appreciation. The main point is we teach our clients specific strategies on how to increase their rents by $100 to $200 or more each month from each house.

7. *Do I still have to fix leaky faucets or clogged toilets?*
You can if you want to, but I don't. My agreement states that the tenant/purchaser is responsible for minor repairs. Remember, they are buying this home. They should maintain it. A minor repair is defined as anything under a certain dollar amount. Our contracts state that the tenant is responsible for the first $200 of repairs in each month. We treat it just like a deductible for insurance purposes.

8. *How do I get started?*
The first step would be to become an Income for Life Member. Fax your FREE trial form at the end of the book. Once you are a member, we will help you each step of the way until you have a large check in your hands from your tenant/buyer for their up-front payment. This includes helping you with our special investor 5% down payment program.

9. *How much do your clients and members pay for your services?*
In the majority of the cases, the Income for Life member receives our team's services for free. Because we are

licensed Realtors, we can charge the seller of the property a commission to be paid out of their sales proceeds.

10 Autopilot Tips to Remember

1. Receive a higher monthly cash flow during the Rent To Own program. Rents can be higher by 10% to 20%.

2. Receive a large non-refundable up-front option down payment at beginning of the program.

3. Huge demand by tenants for Rent To Own programs makes it easier to pick a good tenant.

4. Less maintenance and management is required because the tenant is renting to own. Tenant is responsible for the first $200 of repairs in the home during the lease period.

5. The buyout price to the tenant is based upon the future market value before monthly credits are earned. This means you get to keep the increase in value during the program.

6. Trade one home for two homes, which doubles your monthly positive cash flow.

7. The tenant must pay on or before the first to earn their monthly credit. If they pay on the second, they have lost the monthly credit for that month. This provides a strong positive incentive for them to pay on timc.

8. You keep tax benefits during the rent-to-own period (i.e., the tax loss from depreciation).

53

9. If the tenant doesn't purchase the property, all monies paid are considered rent with no refund of the monthly credit. Start a new Rent To Own program with new tenant with a higher rent, a new option down payment and a higher future buyout price.

10. Consider a five year adjustable rate mortgage when buying an investment. A five year adjustable mortgage rate locks you in at a lower fixed interest rate for the first five years. In the sixth year, the rate will adjust based upon the prevailing rates at that time. However, you will probably not even own the home by the sixth year because it will have been sold to your tenant. But even if you do still own the house by some small chance, you should be able to refinance the property at a very favorable rate because of the equity built up by five years of appreciation.

---

*Please discuss with your tax accountant any 1031 deferred tax plans or capital gains exemptions before entering into a Rent To Own program.

Now for a strictly Canadian perspective...

In the early stages of my investing career I focused on the more common types of investments. Both approaches (Buy, Fix, Sell and Long Term Holding) proved to be profitable but I thought there MUST be a better way.

I then started to invest in Rent to Own homes in Ontario and realized that this really did combine the best parts of real estate investing. Few hassles, tax benefits, upfront cash, possible appreciation and cash flow!

However, there were some of my own mental hurdles I had to overcome when I began using this approach. I was used to renting properties so when I worked out the monthly payment that I would have to receive to make the profit acceptable to me, I thought it was way off the mark.

I was stuck in the landlord mentality. I hadn't yet been able to get my mind around some of the differences between a 'Rent to Own' and a regular 'Rental'.

Would someone really pay me higher than market rent to get into my property? And would they also pay me thousands of dollars in upfront cash?

Then on my very first Rent to Own home I was able to find a tenant/buyer that paid me $250 more than the market rent at that time! Other investors and realtors in the area thought it was impossible, but I had done it. And it happened a few short weeks after I closed on the property.

This is when I began to understand that the approach is not about renting it is about home ownership.

When we work with our members in Oakville, Ontario many of them come from more common real estate investment methods and face some of the same mental hurdles that I had to overcome.

Once you overcome your own limiting beliefs the sky is the limit. We thought we had reached the top monthly payment possible in that particular Rent to Own market (this one was in Hamilton, Ontario and we work with our members to invest throughout Southwestern Ontario). However, not to be out done, some of our clients that took advantage of the member training we provide were able to get even higher monthly payments. As much as $400/month higher!

Also, our upfront payments from tenant/buyers have reached as high as $10,000. That's $10,000 that you receive from a tenant before you even hand over the keys to the home. When you consider that this typically happens within weeks after closing on the home your return on investment is quick and large!

I can still see doubting eyes when working with our members investing in Rent to Own properties. But that all changes when they find their first tenant/buyer. The question then quickly goes from "Can I really do this?" to "How many of these can I do?"

The demand for Rent to Own homes is very strong in any community that we have researched. There are willing and able tenant/buyers available everywhere. It is hard to pigeon hole what the typical prospect would look like because I have seen it vary so widely.

We have helped young couples get into their first home, divorcees looking to restart their life, and people that have sold their current home due to financial distress that did not want to have to move into a rental unit. We have even helped people that could qualify for a mortgage but because of challenged credit the rate was so high that it made much more financial sense to go with a Rent to Own program.

These are all people that do not want to rent. They are attracted by the fact that part of their monthly payment is being used towards the purchase price. They see it as a chance to move themselves forward. The number one reason most tenants provide when looking for Rent to Own homes is, "We're tired of throwing away money on rent'.

One other important point is that when investing in Rent to Own homes, you are investing in 'nice homes in nice areas'. This is critical. Good homes attract good people. And knowing this is like knowing a magic money making secret that makes you money.

We aren't offering typical homes or even those that are a bit worn to our possible tenants. We focus on the top 10% of homes on the street. This is important to fulfill the dream of home ownership. People don't dream of a house that needs work, they dream of the home that sparkles and shines. If you offer this, you have positioned yourself differently than many investors.

The importance of creating a win/win environment for everyone is a great one. I have worked with countless investors and tenants who were both extremely excited about the home. The investor is happy because they will be generating a great return on their capital and their client is also extremely excited to be given this opportunity. I have received numerous messages from both parties giving me thanks. That is truly the best thing that can happen to me on any given day.

When you start out a tenant relationship on this level it drastically changes the positioning. There is commitment to take care of the home and pay the rent on time and there is a reason for them to do it.

Once you begin to understand all the advantages of Rent to Own investing the only limits on the numbers are the ones you place on them.

5

The 10/5/10 Investment Strategy

Before you start to look for a home to invest in, it might be
helpful for you to understand a simple investing formula for
you to use with your investments. Many investors ask us how
to make maximum profits on their real estate investments. To
help with that question, we recommend a simple 10/5/10
investing philosophy to our clients.

The 10/5/10 Philosophy is simple...

- Buy a home 10% below its true market value
- Use a special 5% down payment investor loan program
- Sell the home at 10% more than today's true market value

Well, let's pick this apart a little bit. *The big picture is that you
set yourself up to earn a minimum of 400% on your real estate
investment.* If you stick with me, I will show you how this
works. You actually profit from two avenues with this formula.
The first way you profit is between the purchase price of 10%
below market value and the sale price of 10% above market
value. I refer to this profit avenue as the:

<u>The 20% Price Spread....</u>

Here is a quick example to clarify this point: Assume you
identify a home that has a true value of $100,000. You are
able to use various negotiating strategies to negotiate the
purchase price down to $90,000. If you were now able to sell

59

the home for 10% above today's true value of $100,000 for $110,000, you would earn 20% profit on the spread between $90,000 and $110,000. My guess is that you are probably asking yourself, how do I sell this home for 10% above today's true value of $100,000?

Here is how! You offer the home to a tenant/buyer on a two-year rent-to-own program. Your buyer will have the option to buy your home during the lease at the value at the end of two years. Remember today's true value is $100,000. In my area homes are appreciating at around 5% a year. At the end of year one, this example home would be worth $105,000 ($100,000 * 1.05%). At the end of year two, the home would be worth $110,250 ($105,000 * 1.05%). The value at the end of year two is $110,250 compared to the $90,000 that you paid for the home, for a profit of $20,250. Now take your profit of $20,250 and divide it by $90,000 to calculate your return on investment percentage. If I did the math right, your return was 22.5%. That's not too bad! **In most cases, your return on investment percentage is substantially higher.** And if you're in a hot area where the appreciation is more than 5%, this strategy is considerably more powerful to implement.

Leverage is the Real Key

Above, we discussed the first way you profit through the 20% price spread. Now we will focus on the second way you profit—by leveraging your money. When you purchase an investment by borrowing a portion of the purchase price, you leverage your money. In essence, you super charge your actual out-of-pocket investment by using other people's money, the lender's, to increase your overall return on investment.

More than likely, you obtained a mortgage on this home for most of the $90,000 purchase price. Let's assume that you bought this home with a special 5% down payment program. Many lenders offer 10% down investor loans programs. In this example, your mortgage would be $85,500 (price of $90,000 less 5% down payment) and your investment out of your pocket is $4,500.

For an investment of $4,500 you now control a $100,000 home. That is massive leverage. Understand that if you invest more money into this home with a larger down payment, your rate of return decreases.

Let's now calculate your <u>real</u> return on investment including the supercharged effects of leverage. Profit from the 20% price spread above of $20,250 divided by your actual out-of-pocket cash investment of $4,500 for a whopping 450% return. Notice that I haven't even factored in any of the other income streams that you would receive such as positive cash flow, tax benefits, or equity build up as your mortgage payment is made.

The reason your return is so high under this investing philosophy is because you are creating a massive amount of income with a very small financial investment. To help you see the power of leverage more clearly, compare the two investing approaches below:

INVESTMENT ONE:

1. Buy a $100,000 home using a 25% down payment.

2. At the end of year one, the home appreciates to $105,000.

3. The increase in value is $5,000 divided by your investment of $25,000.

Rate of Return at End of Year One is 20%

INVESTMENT TWO:

1. Buy the same $100,000 home using a 5% down payment.

2. At the end of year one, the home appreciates to $105,000.

3. The increase in value is $5,000 divided by your investment of $5,000.

Rate of Return at End of Year One is 100%

As noted above, the same property produced five times the rate of return by structuring your investment with a smaller out-of-pocket investment. By using more of the lender's money and less of your own, you dramatically increase your overall rate of return.

Can you now see how the 10/5/10 formula can make you wealthy? In almost every investment using the 10/5/10 philosophy, your return will be a minimum of 400%. Let me challenge you a little bit now with this thought…

Try to Invest with an ERROR in Mind

In the 10/5/10 investment philosophy, you earn a minimum of 400% on your investments. That is a pretty good investment right? It definitely beats the profit of 20% in the price spread.

What if you bought this home using $0.00 of your own money?

What would your real return on investment be using 100% financial leverage? Well, you take your profits of $22,250 and divide it by, well $0.00 and your return is *(error)*. I actually got an *error* on my calculator when I calculated this. I honestly love that. I love when I try to calculate one of my investing client's rates of return and I get an error on my calculator. When you put no money into an investment, the return on investment is so high that it can't be calculated! In college they told me that the return was infinite. Whatever you want to call it, it works for me. My guess is that it works for you too!

To learn a few strategies on how to invest in real estate without using your money for the down payment, read on!

Many people want to invest and incorrectly think that they need thousands of dollars in their bank account to get started. For my first real estate investment, I borrowed the down payment from my Mom! Thanks Mom, I couldn't have done it without you. Remember, if you purchased an investment with zero of your own money, your return is infinite. I paid my Mom back in monthly installments with a 12% interest rate. It was a win/win deal because my mom earned a nice return on her loan to me and I earned an infinite return on my investment. Be sure that the monthly rental income you receive from your property covers both payments and you are okay. When I say both payments, I mean the payment on your loan to the bank and the payment on your down payment loan.

Yes, this takes a little effort and some creativity, but it does work and you can do it. In fact, here are a few ways for you to buy properties with none of your own money! The key for you to realize is that in most cases, you will need to invest a down payment to acquire an investment property. However, it doesn't necessarily have to be your money. There are many ways for you to get started. Some ideas are:

1. Buy the home and move into it for a short period of time. Our lending partner has several loan programs that require zero down payments. The catch is that the buyer must occupy the home. Move into it for a short period and then rent it out using a Rent-to-Own program and then buy another home to move into. Every home that you move into may be purchased for no money down if your credit meets the lenders guidelines. I personally have helped one client buy eight properties with hardly any money out of their pocket with this technique.

2. If you own a home now, get an equity line and use some of the credit line for the down payment. Understand that the rent you get from your rent-to-own home should cover the credit line repayment and the mortgage on your new rental home. You would be investing your home's equity for infinite returns.

3. Consider a partner that has funds available to invest, or equity in their home. Structure a partnership where you find the properties and manage them. Your partner puts up the money and you split the profits. This would be a win/win partnership. However, a word of caution on partnerships. You want to make sure there is a clear understanding of how to get out of the partnership. In our Income for Life Monthly Newsletter, we share tips

for partnership agreements to ensure that everyone understands what happens in different situations.

4. Borrow your down payment from your other sources. I know this might sound scary, but many people have money invested at very low rates of return and they would be happy to make more on their investment. I don't recommend that you borrow to buy a home to move into. I do recommend borrowing the money to invest it at substantially higher rates of return.

Now for a strictly Canadian perspective...

Canadians are skeptical.

The first time I shared the idea that you could by an investment property with 5% down the group of friends I was with couldn't believe it. For some reason Canadians think you have to put down 25% or even 35% down to buy an investment property. Most people just don't know where to look. It's not like we're taught any of this stuff in school.

The 10/5/10 strategy works here in Canada as well. There are mortgage programs available for 5% down payments, 10% down payments and 15% down payments on investment properties. There are even some for 0% down investments. Some banks have been offering their good clients zero down investment mortgages for years but wouldn't advertise them to the general public.

Start asking around. You'll quickly learn of the new mortgage programs open to investors. And we're in for a real treat: As the U.S mortgage insurance companies enter Canada, we'll have more competition offering these mortgage programs.

We're already starting to see the beginning of this. One of the large U.S. mortgage insurers has already announced their plans to enter into Canada. This quickly caused an existing Canadian mortgage insurer to offer a brand new 10% down investment program. And a few short months later another mortgage insurer announced a 5% and even 0% down payment investment mortgage program. Long live competition!

One of the key things brought up in this chapter is the idea of leverage. When you understand the power of leverage this investing strategy really looks attractive.

In Canada we often use a 10/10/10 strategy because a 10% down investment mortgage is rather easy to qualify for and has excellent interest rates.

The stock market has historical returns that are often quoted and compared to real estate. Depending on what index and date ranges are used, the stock market may show a historical rate of return in between 7% and 13%. Through the use of leverage with real estate, you can EASILY beat this.

By controlling a $250,000 home with 10% down ($25,000) you dramatically increase your rate of return. When using Rent to Own programs, it is not uncommon to expect at least a 100% return on your investment over a two year period. That's the type of return on investment that generates some real cash flow!

Let's break it down:

Step One: Buy a $250,000 home. A nice home in a nice area. Not a fixer upper.

Step Two: Lock in profits by appreciating the home upon placing a tenant/buyer using a two year Rent to Own program. We typically use a 5.7% appreciation rate per year when we sell the home to a tenant/buyer on a rent to own program. However, let's use 5% to be conservative.

Purchase Price = $250,000
+ 5% after Year 1 ($12,500)
+ 5% after Year 2 ($13,125)
Sale Price = **$275,625**
Increase = $25,625

That's over 100% return and we have not included monthly positive cash flow from the property or the equity build-up over the two years.

In this example you have earned a profit of $25,625 and you get your original 10% down payment of $25,000 back when you sell the house. So on closing you receive a total of $50,625.

And now that 5% and 0% down payments have become more common in Canada you can put less money down and earn an even higher return on your investment. In the above example if you had put only 5% down ($12,500) your return on investment is over 200%.

67

There are other things to consider in this example. Things like credits, mortgage insurance fees and closing costs. However, when you structure your investment properly you can incorporate all of these and still secure 100% and 200% returns.

There are people doing this right in your own backyard here in Canada! You likely didn't even know it was going on.

Now you know.

6

The MOST Important Key to Your Success in Real Estate Investing

If I had to rank what was the most important factor in determining your success investing in real estate, it would be selecting the RIGHT property. Have you ever known anyone that tells terrible stories about owning real estate as an investment? Almost everyone has heard of horror stories that real estate investors have encountered. I have a personal friend that owned 44 units. In just one of his properties, a 12-unit building, the tenants stole all of the furnaces and copper plumbing. The average cost of a new furnace is $1,500, so that was an expensive problem. Needless to say, my friend doesn't own any real estate investments today. He got so burned and burned out from his investments that he gave it up completely.

My guess is that many of these problems occur because the investor bought a property that attracts problem tenants. Here is the biggest tip I can give anyone about real estate investing:

> **THE RIGHT PROPERTY ATTRACTS THE RIGHT TENANT**

On the flip side, the wrong property attracts the wrong tenants or no tenants at all. Understand that when I say tenant, I mean a tenant/buyer in a rent-to-own program. Or for that matter any tenant. The rule rings true for every type of property, commercial, multi-family and single-family. Each type of property can attract a bad tenant or a good tenant.

I used to own multi-family homes because I thought that I would have more positive monthly cash flow each month. What I learned was if you own multi-family properties, you have to invest a significant amount of time to manage them. As I have already explained, time is your most important asset. I quickly realized that for every unit you own, you have a part-time job. If you own a four-family apartment building, you just took on four part-time jobs.

Take a moment and picture a four-family investment property in your mind. What type of tenant do you think would want to rent an apartment in this property? The reality is that a multi-family home attracts tenants that are more transient. Their jobs change quite frequently, they are in and out of relationships quickly and they don't usually stay in one place for a long time. Their income isn't stable and they don't have many responsibilities in life. Because this is the type of tenant that looks to rent an apartment, you as the investor are forced to rent to them. You have an apartment building full of unstable tenants!

If you have unstable tenants, you are forced to spend more time managing your properties. In one of my two family homes, I rented to a young couple who were engaged. They had a beautiful baby daughter. He worked as a chef in a local bar. As you could imagine, he changed restaurants quite frequently. Well, someone cheated in the relationship and she moved out taking his daughter with her. In order to help him pay the rent, he had a friend move into the other bedroom. Understand that this happened without my approval. Now I had a unit with two guys that were partying all the time. This isn't what I had signed up for. My other tenant in this home was a single girl who didn't party.

You could probably guess that the police were called quite frequently. When the police were called, I was called. It was a very draining experience for me. However, I am glad that it happened because I learned a great deal from it.

What I learned from owning multi-family homes is that you have to rent your properties more frequently because your tenants move a great deal. When someone moves out, it costs you substantially. Here are just some of your costs:

1. You have to clean any mess.

2. You have to repair all of the broken items.

3. You have to possibly replace carpet or tile.

4. You have to paint.

5. You have to pay to advertise.

6. You have to invest time to show it.

7. You LOSE rental income while it's vacant.

8. You run the risk of getting a new tenant who won't pay the rent and has to be evicted.

I have watched many investors buy a property simply because they thought they found a great deal. Unfortunately, the great deal was only surface deep. They found a seller that was flexible on price, and/or terms and they bought the home, or the home was dirt cheap to buy. The problem these investors found was their "deal" wasn't a property that attracted good tenants. These investors struggled because they couldn't find good stable tenants to live in their properties. As an investor, you don't want to be in this situation. Here is why:

1. Your home will sit vacant and you will make the full monthly mortgage payment out of your pocket.

2. You will get desperate and select the wrong tenant/buyer and be forced to evict the tenant down the road.

Let's take a step back for a minute. Ask yourself this very important question before you invest:

<u>What type of tenant/buyer do I want to attract?</u>

How did you answer this question? For me, I like to attract tenants that meet these three criteria:

1. Are stable in their lives and jobs

2. Have the ability to pay on time

3. Will appreciate and care for the home during the rental period

After thinking about the type of tenants you would like to attract, ask yourself the next big question:

<u>What home, in what location, would this ideal tenant want to live in?</u>

The better you are at answering these two questions, the more profitable your real estate investing will be. Remember, if you offer a Rent-to-Own program, your tenant/buyer must want to own the home, not just rent it. They want to make a long-term commitment. They want to make the home better by investing their time and money into making improvements. They want to be proud of their home. They want to raise their family in the home. They want to make friends with the neighbors and have cookouts.

I have found that nice homes, in nice areas, attract nice tenants. These tenants are stable, have good jobs and love the homes. Here are some of my findings on the best home.

1. The larger the better! Understand that someone looking for a rent-to-own single-family home is more than likely moving from a small, cramped apartment. They are hungry for space. I have learned that the larger the home you have to offer, the more demand you will have. Also, if your home is large enough, your tenants will not feel the need to move to get more space, which increases the probability of them purchasing your home during the lease period. Because of the larger size, it will be easier for you to rent your home, which means you will create an income stream faster.

2. A good neighborhood. The ideal tenant will want to live in a home in a nice area. If they feel that their safety is in jeopardy, they will not want to stay in your home. If it is a Rent-to-Own program, your tenant/buyer will want a good neighborhood for their kids to play. They want to make friends with the neighbors. They want tree-lined streets and block parties.

3. Curb appeal. What feeling will your prospective tenant/buyer have when they see the home from the street? Will they be proud of the home when their friends and family come to visit? If your home looks bad from the street, it will be very hard for you to rent it to a good tenant. Ugly homes repel good tenants. Nice homes attract good tenants. Ugly homes attract bad tenants. Birds of a feather flock together.

4. Condition. If you were able to find a home that ranks well on the three findings above, you don't need to be as concerned about the interior condition of the home. Fresh paint and new carpeting are inexpensive and create immediate results to help excite your tenant/buyers. In fact, I have rented homes to good tenants that needed new carpeting and paint. I was able to find good tenants because I got numbers one, two, and three above correct!

Other things to look for in an investment property?

I usually recommend to my clients that they look for a home that has newer updates. The most expensive items in a house to replace or repair are the roof, windows, concrete (driveway), furnace and a wet basement. We specifically look for homes with newer roofs, windows, concrete, furnace and air conditioning. In some cases, if we find the right home, I will negotiate to have the seller replace something to prevent my investor client from having an unexpected large repair bill.

The best part about the Rent to Own program, if you decide to try this with your investments, is that you will not own the home for a very long time. At most, you will only own the home for four or five years. The major items in the home—

such as the roof, windows, furnace, hot-water tank and air conditioning—usually last for 11 to 12 years at a minimum. When you're looking to buy a home for a Rent to Own program, you really only need to be concerned with the remaining life of the major mechanicals at the time of purchase. If they have seven or eight years of life remaining, you probably won't need to invest much money to maintain them during your ownership.

Here is the funny thing...

The funny thing is that the homes that attract the best tenant/buyers are the same homes that have the highest increases in value over time. Homes that don't attract good tenant/buyers don't increase in value by the same percentages. A home's value is based upon the number of buyers that want to buy it outright. The greater the demand for a home, the higher the price! Just consider California, Florida and many other hot areas. The home prices are double or triple what they are in other parts of the country. This is because of the fierce buyer demand.

If there are only a few buyers that want to buy the home outright, the home's value will not increase very much over time. So, not only are you buying nice homes that will be hassle free investments because of the quality of the people that will want to rent them, but you're also buying homes that provide the greatest return on your investment.

Here is an example of what I mean: First, there is Joe who buys a $65,000 home to put on a Rent to Own program. At the end of two years, with annual appreciation of 3% a year, his home's value increases by $3,958 to $68,958. Along comes

Susan who buys a $140,000 home to put on a rent to own program. At the end of two years, with annual appreciation of 5% a year, her home's value increases by $14,350 to $154,350. Notice that Susan made $10,392 MORE than Joe in two years without doing any extra work. Because her home was located in a nice neighborhood, it appreciated at a higher annual rate of 5% vs. 3% in poor neighborhood.

Did you catch that? She made more money without working any harder.

You can earn more money with less work. By buying the right investment property, you will have less hassle renting it and managing it because it will attract quality tenants. In addition, your home will grow in value at a faster rate. You probably have heard the old saying that you should work smarter, not harder. This is a prime example of how to get the maximum value out of your time.

Before I close out this chapter, understand that there are different types of homes for different investing strategies. For example, I invested in a small two-bedroom condo. This condo is about 900 square feet. I tried to offer the home on a Rent-to-Own program. It was very difficult to find a tenant. I finally realized that nobody had dreams of owning such a small condo. When I changed my approach to offering the condo for rent under the Section 8 Housing program, my phone rang off the hook and the property rented very quickly. I now plan on keeping this condo forever and collecting my rent checks from the government each month. Autopilot income!

I just wonder…

In the beginning of this chapter, I mentioned a friend who had 44 units at one time. This is the guy that got so burned out that he sold all of his real estate investments. I often wonder, how his life would be today, had he owned 10 nice homes in nice areas back then? Would he still own real estate as an investment? If you get burned out on your real estate investments, you will want out of your investments. Each investment you make is like a little money tree that pays you dollar bills. If you get out of your real estate investments, you in essence chop down your little money tree. So plant your money tree in a place where it will be safe from everyone, including you. Invest in homes that attract the good tenants!

Now for a strictly Canadian perspective...

"Nice homes attract nice tenants".

The first time I heard that it was a big 'ah-hah' moment for me. Of course good homes attract good tenants, how obvious. I'm not sure why hearing this is such a 'eureka' moment for people, but it often is.

When I started investing in real estate, my wife handled a lot of the communications and paper work for us. After picking up our first Rent to Own property she wondered out loud why she never heard from the family in that home. They just continued to pay their rent every month. We wouldn't hear from them for months at a time.

Sometimes I almost felt compelled to call them and check that they were actually still living there! A couple of times I secretly drove by to check that the house was still standing. I just couldn't believe that using a Rent to Own program on a nice house could be this easy. It was great! Immediately my mantra became "Nice homes, nice areas," and I can validate that there is truth to this idea. Nice homes do attract nice people.

Of course, nothing is guaranteed and perhaps at some point I will have some issue with a Rent to Own tenant, but from my own experiences and from the majority of experiences that I have witnessed it's clear that using Rent to Own is a highly sophisticated strategy to invest in real estate.

But what about cash flow?

Often people will approach me and discuss their idea to rent a 3-plex or a 4-plex to begin their investing adventure. When I drill them on their reasons it usually revolves around cash flow. They feel that by investing in a small multi-unit rental property they can generate enough cash flow to cover the mortgage, property tax and insurance payments.

Well now that you know about rent to own programs you have another way to do the same thing! You can achieve positive cash flow and have fewer hassles in the process. You will invest less time on the property and have higher and faster returns on your investment. What more can you ask for?

Can you Rent to Own an ugly home?

Recently I have witnessed some Rent to Own programs offered in the Greater Toronto Area that are definitely not following the "Nice homes, nice areas" mantra I mention above.

Rent to Own has a lot of advantages and I'm certain that with the obvious lack of competition for these types of programs you can easily find a tenant for an ugly home using a Rent to Own program. Just remember that the quality of your investing experience will likely be tied to the quality of your home.

Also, I have found that the good homes will find good tenants faster and attract higher rents and higher up-front payments. So, although it may be natural to look for the best "deal" it may not be your most effective approach.

Here's why....

Many first time investors are most concerned with the amount of time it will take to find a tenant for their home. However, during the buying process they remain focused on the best "deal".

I can tell you with confidence that searching for the best deal will likely mean that your purchase isn't the best house on the street and may even be one of the worst houses on the street.

As a result you'll have to spending money on things like fresh paint and carpet. Outgoing cash flow is not my favourite thing.

Your home will be vacant during this process and it will take longer to find a good tenant for the home. Do you really think a good tenant is looking for one of the worst houses on the street?

So although we have all been trained to look for the best "deal", start to focus on looking for the best returns on your time and your money.

By buying a good home for slightly under market value you will have nothing to do before you offer it on a Rent to Own program. You likely won't even have to sweep the porch.

Doing things this way means you are buying into demand. There are always people looking for good starter homes. It took me a long time to realize that buying homes, fixing them up and then selling them is actually speculation. You are speculating that someone will buy the home from you at a higher price.

I know there are people in my own backyard that are actively looking for their own home but have some circumstances that are preventing them from buying today. By using Rent to Own programs I am buying into demand. This is a big point - buy into demand.

Most investors doing this do not do a single thing before they rent out the home. They are investors, not contractors.

Remember, good homes rent out fast and for more money upfront.

Say it with me, "Nice homes, nice areas!"

7

How to Find and Buy Nice Homes Below Value

I have explained how important the right property is to your success in investing. The right property attracts the right tenant! This chapter will show you how to find and acquire the right property below market value. You don't have to find a home that is 20% or 30% below market value. My target is to shoot for 10% below market value, as discussed in the section on the 10/5/10 investing formula. Many investors make the mistake of trying to get homes too far below their market value. They waste way too much time with this approach. When your focus is to buy homes at 90% of their value, you can find many more homes to choose from. In fact, it takes us only about five hours on average to find a nice single-family home for our investors to buy.

What I have found is that half of the battle in investing is identifying a home that has all of your key parameters and can be purchased below value. The problem is that almost every buyer is looking for the same thing. So, in most cases you are competing with every other buyer to find these homes below value. Typically when you find a property that is below value, you are in competition to buy the home with other buyers or investors. When I say competition, I mean that there are other offers from other buyers on the same property. To win the multiple-offer game, in most cases, you need to be the highest bidder. Obviously, when you are forced to pay more for the

81

home, your profits are reduced accordingly. My suggestion to you is to stop putting yourself in this situation. Make a decision today to stop….

Competing with Other Buyers for Homes

Here is a real life situation that happened in my office recently. (As you probably already know, we are a real estate brokerage that specializes in helping real estate investors find and acquire investment properties.) One of my team members was working with an investor client who was looking for a home that could be purchased below value. They spotted a home that was just listed. They viewed the home the same day it was put on the market. The investor recognized the value and made an offer that was over asking price. Before the seller accepted our client's offer, several additional offers were submitted on this home for the seller to consider. The seller selected a different offer, and our client lost the home. Our investor client lost this home because of competition from other buyers. You can imagine their frustration at the loss, considering that they acted very quickly and made an offer over the seller's asking price.

There is a better way to approach your real estate investing that will virtually eliminate your competition when looking to buy a home.

The first step to eliminating the competition is to set up and follow an automatic property filtering system. The system you should follow is one that will highlight properties that would make the best candidates for further investigation. When I say a filtering system, the picture I compare it to is a website that performs screens of the stock market. If you invest in the stock market, you probably have visited a few websites that will screen the entire universe of stocks and provide you with a short list of stocks that you could investigate further. These stock screens search all of the listed stocks looking for certain criteria. If a stock hits all of your criteria, it has passed the screen and is worthy of your time. You can then just focus on studying the short list of stocks that pass the screen instead of the entire universe of stocks. As you can imagine, there are many benefits to using an automatic filtering system.

One benefit is that a screening system provides you with incredible focus. Many investors get distracted and bogged down because they are overwhelmed with properties. They are not sure where they should be spending their time. Another benefit to a filtering system is the enormous time savings. The system automatically focuses your time on the absolute best candidates. You don't have to waste time looking at homes that don't have the potential of being purchased below value.

Use a Filtering System to Save Yourself Time and Aggravation

The starting place to your system would be the entire population of homes in your specific geographic area. Select an area that is within a close proximity to your home. The reason I recommend investing close to your home is because it will save you a significant amount of time in showing and managing your property during your ownership. If you have to drive a long distance, you probably won't show your home very aggressively, nor will you do as good a job of managing it.

For most people, the next step that they take is the wrong one. They try to identify the homes that are offered below value within their geographic area. This is where all of the competition occurs. This is exactly what everyone else is doing. Don't do this!!! The place that most investors go to find homes in their area way below value is sheriff sales. They believe they can just walk down to the courthouse and buy a home $50,000 below value. For the record, it does happen, but not as often as the TV commercials would have you believe. Sheriff sale homes are sold at an auction. An auction means there are several other buyers bidding on the same home. Who wins in an auction? The seller! Don't waste your time on homes that other buyers will be bidding on. It is a complete waste of your time. Spend your time on homes that no other buyers are bidding on!

Consider the following screens to identify homes that can be purchased below value….

Your First Filtering Screen: Motivated sellers!

In every market around the world, a certain percentage of all sellers will be motivated. Motivated sellers are motivated because of personal circumstances such as a divorce, a job loss, a vacant home, two mortgage payments, job relocation and so on… These homes are not usually listed for sale with an asking price that is below value. Because these homes are not listed for sale with below-market asking prices, other investors don't even inquire about them. Other investors are too busy looking at the lower priced homes or at the sheriff sales.

In the paragraph above, there is a very valuable piece of information. The majority of motivated sellers have their homes listed for sale at the home's market value or higher. Just because their home is listed for sale with a price at market value, doesn't mean they will sell the home at market value. motivated sellers will sell their homes below market value. They just don't list them for sale at a price below market value.

The best way to identify motivated sellers is to screen for homes that have been on the market for longer periods of time.

As I mentioned above, motivated sellers are motivated because of personal circumstances. Many sellers create a personal circumstance that makes them motivated. The best example I can give you is to consider this scenario:

Mr. Smith and his family have outgrown their current home. So they started looking for a new home, but didn't think that they would find anything that they liked so quickly. As usually happens, Mr. Smith and his family stumbled across the perfect home for their family. Because they didn't want to lose this lovely home, they bought it without first selling their current home. Because they now have purchased this new home, they list their current home for sale. Unfortunately, Mr. Smith makes the same mistake that the majority of sellers make and he overprices his current home. Because Mr. Smith is now on the hook for his new home's payment and his current home's payment, he has become a motivated seller. In essence, Mr. Smith created a personal circumstance that has made him motivated.

In most real estate markets around the world, a home that is priced properly will sell within the first 30 days of being on the market. New home listings have the most buyer traffic during the first 30 days on the market. After the first 30 days, the listing is old news, so to speak. The reason why the listing becomes old news is because the majority of the buyers looking in that area and price range have already considered the home. If the seller overprices their home in the beginning, the majority of the buyer traffic will pass on the home because of its pricing. So, in essence, the seller has missed the boat by offering an unattractive price during the best period of the marketing time. After 30 days on the market, the only way for a seller to increase the buyer traffic is to drop their asking price. However, at this point it usually is too late.

Quick Tip: When you are selling a home, do not overprice the home in the beginning! I promise you that it will cost you substantially in your ultimate selling price. Price the home attractively right at the very beginning and sell it within the first 30 days. Don't become a motivated seller!

When I say longer market times, I mean homes that have been on the market longer than average. In our office, we track the average number of days homes remain on the market for sale. If you were thinking of investing in a three bedroom colonial home in Bakersville, USA we would be analyzing:

1. The AVERAGE sale price of three bedroom colonials in Bakersville over the last 12 months

2. The AVERAGE number of days a three bedroom colonial in Bakersville is on the market

This analysis might show that homes are on the market for 67 days. With this information, I can narrow your search of homes to homes on the market 67 days or longer. When you are looking at homes with longer market times, you are more than likely one of the only buyers looking at the home.

Remember, the listing is old news to the majority of buyers because they have already walked through or considered this home. This is the single best way an investor can eliminate other buyers competing with them for an investment.

Now, put yourself in the seller's shoes. Their home has been on the market for three months. They have had to keep their home clean, they have had to be inconvenienced in their lifestyles to show the home, and they are getting fed up with the process. In addition, in most cases, they are starting to doubt if their home will actually sell because they don't have any offers to consider. Or maybe they had a lower offer earlier that they rejected and are having second thoughts on. Can you see how this is the best type of seller to be working with? These sellers are usually incredibly flexible on their price because of the personal circumstance that they have created for themselves. In addition, they do not have any other options because no other buyers have shown any interest!

I am going to share one more secret that will help you immensely. When a home is listed for sale with a Realtor and the home has been on the market for some time. Not only do you have a motivated seller on your hands, but you also will have a motivated Realtor. Most listing contracts are for three, four or six months. If the home hasn't sold and the listing contract is about to expire, the Realtor will lose the listing. This Realtor has worked for several months, investing their time and money in marketing and showing the home. They will usually settle for a smaller piece of the pie to recover their costs, than no pie at all. What I mean is that they will more than likely be willing to lower their commission to get the home sold. If they lower their listing commission, the seller can afford to sell the home to you at a lower price. In many of the homes our investor clients acquire, we negotiate to have the listing agent reduce their commissions. This allows my clients to buy the homes at an even lower price.

<u>Longer Market Time Increases Motivation</u>

Sometimes we recommend having our clients wait on making an offer on a home. If we identify a good home that has short market time, we may suggest to the client that the home could be purchased for a lower price if we waited a month or so to pursue it. This is a specific strategy that does work. However, you can and will lose some nice homes by letting them stay on the market. The payoff on the homes that remain on the market is no buyer competition and the possibility of a seller who is a little more motivated.

Your Second Filtering Screen: Vacant Homes

As you can imagine, a vacant home is a big liability to whoever owns it. They have to maintain this home by cutting the grass, trimming the bushes, shoveling snow and so on. They have to pay the property taxes, insurance and utilities and mortgage payment. They still have all of the obligations of owning this home without having any benefits. Every month that their home sits on the market without a sale, it costs them more money.

In our offices, we have a searching system that searches for vacant homes. We can specifically look for homes in any area and any price range that are vacant. Realize that a home's vacancy status can change over time. A seller could be living in a home when they first list it for sale and then they could move out in a few weeks. A vacant home is usually a good sign that the seller is motivated.

In our offices, we download each and every week a list of homes advertised in the local newspapers as For Sale By Owner. We keep these weekly files for future follow up to help our clients identify motivated For Sale By Owners. We also try to cross match the list of For Sale By Owner Homes with the public records to see when the seller purchased the home and for what price. We include these details in our weekly list to provide our clients with more information rather than less. If you can identify a home that has been on the market for some time, is vacant and has a low mortgage on it, you should definitely investigate it further.

Your Third Filtering Screen: Search for Key Words

Another way that we identify bargain homes is to search for key words. We search the entire inventory of homes listed for sale with Realtors for certain key words. Here are the top 20 key words that we search for:

1. Priced Below Value

2. Seller Needs Quick Sale

3. Price Reduced

4. SARO (Submit All Reasonable Offers)

5. Appraisal (looking for homes priced below appraisal)

6. Divorce

7. Vacant

8. Motivated seller

9. Desperate

10. Needs (home needing minor work)

11. Bank Owned

12. Foreclosure

13. Estate (a home that is being sold to close out an estate)

14. Fixer Upper

15. Relocation (seller is forced to sell due to a relocation)

16. Power of Sale

17. Auction

18. TLC (many homes are listed as needing "Tender Loving Care")

19. Seller will listen to all offers. Or, All Offers Considered (Some sellers offer a buyer an allowance for closing costs or repairs to the home. I have found that seller's offering an allowance of some sort are motivated.)

20. Negotiable

We have had the computer guys program searching software for us to be able to search for these key terms. The computer screens all of the homes and pulls out any homes that have any of these key words. Once these properties are identified, they are further considered for our investor clients. By using this screen, we pinpoint additional opportunities for finding homes that can be purchased below their market value.

Your Fourth Filtering Screen: Expired Home Listings

These homes can be an absolute gold mine! An expired listing is a home that was listed for sale with a Realtor and didn't sell. The listing contract with the Realtor has expired on this home. For our clients, we have programmed our system to automatically search and download expired listings every day. For homes that match our client's criteria, the system will email us with an update that includes the homes particulars.

In our area, over 50% of the homes listed for sale do not sell the first time that they are on the market. What we have learned to do is to watch and wait for these listings to expire. Because these homes are technically not for sale anymore when they expire, there is absolutely no competition from other buyers. Remember that expired listings are homes where the owner really wants to sell, but hasn't had any luck on the market.

You can attack expired home listings without any other buyer competition!

Those are the four main filtering screens that we use to highlight probable candidates for further consideration. Understand this important point, we layer the filtering screens. What I mean is that we can run the screens on top of each other.

We run each screen to identify the best properties in that particular screen. We then combine all of the best properties from each screen and narrow our list down from that point. With this approach, our clients get to choose from the best homes selected from the best filtering screens.

The whole goal of the screening system is to focus in on properties that might have a motivated seller, properties that you can buy without having to compete with other buyers. If you would like to have access to our system and these property screening tools, fax us your new Income for Life Membership form at the of the end book. The system was designed so we can notify our clients of the homes that pass these screens.

From the above information in this chapter, you will probably see that the best way to approach your real estate investing is to do the exact opposite that everyone else is doing. Stop looking for the lowest priced homes, because that's what everyone else is doing. My mother used to tell me, "Work Smarter, Not Harder." My hope is that you can learn from these strategies to work smarter and save yourself a tremendous amount of time.

Now for a strictly Canadian perspective…

One of the most common things you will hear from seasoned investors is that you make money in real estate when you buy the home. Not when you sell it, when you *buy* it. This is because the most important part of investing is finding the property that will allow you to make money. Anyone can find a property for sale but finding one that will be a good investment is considerably more time consuming.

When investing in an active market it is important to be knowledgeable of the homes on the market. Many investors start in their real estate careers while still holding down full time work. This will drastically limit the amount of time he or she will have available to be able to search through home listings to determine what is a good investment. Often by the time an investor even gets around to seeing the home it will already be sold.

Much of the information available to investors can be out of date. Our software is consistently updated with all the homes on the market and any changes made to them (ex. asking price). Our team is consistently scanning this system to ensure we are up to date with all the available opportunities.

The types of searches mentioned earlier will help you identify 'motivated' sellers. These people have a need to sell and may be willing to negotiate very favourable terms. However, not all these homes are going to be good investments. That is why it is important to be familiar with the market you are investing in.

We work with our clients to 'crunch the numbers' on each property they invest in. This gives our clients the opportunity to evaluate the potential investment to ensure it will match their investment criteria. We educate them on the market and current conditions to give them as much first hand, real life, information as possible before they move forward.

This is extremely important because sometimes, something as seemingly unimportant as a 2 block difference in location can greatly affect the potential profit on your investment. Always ensure that prior to moving forward, no matter how attractive the price looks, you do your due diligence.

Do a bit of research into the area and what the potential profit might be. Does this match your investment goals? Not every good investment will be for every investor.

Some people are out looking for beat up, run down places to renovate and try to sell for a profit. As we talked about earlier most of the people we work with do not want to be involved in these. However, there are investors that will jump at the opportunity.

It might be those same investors that would not want to buy a nice house in a nice area because they may not understand how to turn it into a cash machine. They may not understand the term 'buying into demand'. This is definitely the key in the investment world.

Using a system to stay on top of the market and the opportunities that arise is important, as is using a system in all parts of your real estate business. Proven systems can allow people to move forward, faster, that trying to reinvent the wheel.

8

The Four-Point Home Search and How It Can Help You Buy Homes Below Value

About the Search

This exclusive four-point home search was developed to give our clients the most comprehensive list of homes that could be purchased, plus assist them in identifying homes that could possibly be purchased below value. This search and the variables that are searched for have been painstakingly developed over years of research and effort.

This home searching software has been programmed to search for several variables throughout the entire real estate market. The software will search for all property types including: single-family homes, multi-family homes, condominiums, new construction and vacant land.

Once we program our software for your specific home buying criteria, it will search minute by minute for homes that could possibly be great values. In reality, the software actually is performing multiple searches for you every minute. This software searches all homes listed by all Realtors, including all real estate companies. This means that the entire population of homes on the market is being searched for you by our software system.

The reason this searching software will be so valuable to you is that it will identify homes that you can purchase for thousands of dollars below value. Here is just one real life success story for you to consider….

"The four-point home search and the Home Selling Team's negotiating strategies helped our family find and buy the home we have been dreaming about for thousands of dollars below the seller's asking price. This system identified an estate home on the lake for sale at $275,000. We just signed final papers last night to purchase this home for $230,000, a $45,000 discount from the asking price." --- Rich Weybrecht

The following information will explain each of the four searches that can be programmed for you and provide you with an example of homes that have been identified by the system. You will see that this home searching system was designed around the four property screens discussed in the previous chapter.

Another great benefit is that many of the homes identified by our software can be purchased with our Special 5% Down Payment Investor Loan Program. Certain properties do not qualify for this 5% down payment program.

SEARCH ONE: The Distressed and Foreclosure Search

This search was designed to specifically find and pinpoint homes that have been through the foreclosure process. These homes may, or may not need a great deal of work. The search looks for homes that have been repossessed in any condition. Some of the factors that this search looks for are:

Bank Owned Homes:
These are homes that the lending bank purchased back from the seller. This happens for various reasons. Understand that banks don't want to own homes. They want to loan money on them. When a bank owns a home, it is considered a liability. Our software specifically looks for homes that are bank owned.

Foreclosed Homes:
These are homes that have been through the complete foreclosure process. They are typically vacant and can be thoroughly inspected by all buyers. Some of these homes will need work to make them livable. Others may not. These homes could be owned by banks or by individuals that are holding them for sale. We can search for all foreclosed homes in your area.

Power of Sales:
While the searching software will look for bank owned homes sometimes they are owned by smaller lenders that can be outside of our area. Power of Sale is more of a Canadian term that is used when a bank is advertising a home for sale. Our searching software will search for all Power of Sale properties and catch additional bank owned homes.

Sellers Facing a Foreclosure:
In some circumstances, homeowners that haven't made their mortgage payments understand that they can prevent the homes foreclosure by selling it before the foreclosure occurs. These homeowners typically offer their homes for sale at attractive prices in hopes to sell them fast and prevent a foreclosure from

hitting their credit reports. These homes will be pinpointed by our searching software.

The Distressed and Foreclosure Search performs each of the above searches minute by minute throughout each day. When the software identifies a match to your home buying criteria, it will automatically email you a notice, including the details of the identified home.

SEARCH TWO: The Motivated seller Search

With this search, the software looks for any hint that the seller of a home is motivated. A motivated seller is important to find for a home buyer, because they usually will sell their home below value. A motivated home seller is usually created by some personal situation. This situation is unique to the seller. In every market place throughout the country, there is always a small percentage of home sellers that are motivated.

A motivated seller will tend to be more flexible on their price and terms, which makes the home a better overall value for you as the buyer. Some of the factors that our software will look for are:

Vacant Homes: A vacant home is a possible sign that the seller is motivated. If the seller has already bought a new home and moved into it, they may be making two mortgage payments. Two mortgage payments every month has a tendency to make the seller motivated.

Divorce Situations: sellers that are going through a divorce typically will want to have their home sold quickly to eliminate both financial and emotional problems. These sellers are more focused on their personal situation than the price and value of their home.

Estate Sales: An estate home is a home whose owner is no longer alive. The estate usually has an executor that is chosen to handle the sale of the home. The executor's role is to sell the home in a timely fashion so that the estate can close. Estate homes may be available below value depending on the situation.

Relocation Situations: A seller that has been relocated because of their job usually wants to have their home sold quickly because they will not be able to manage the home from a long distance. Also, in some relocation situations, the employer may be paying some or all of the seller's moving costs. If the seller is saving thousands of dollars in settlement costs with their sale, they can afford to be more flexible with their asking price.

Financially Motivated sellers: These sellers are motivated because they simply can't afford their home payments any longer. Maybe they have lost their jobs or have some large unexpected bills, but in any case, they need and want to sell their homes quickly. sellers that can't afford their monthly payments usually will sell their homes below value to stop their financial problems.

Homes Priced Below Appraisal: In some situations, sellers have their homes appraised before they put the home on the market. If there is some indication that they have priced their

99

home below their appraisal, our software will pinpoint their home for you.

> When we search for motivated home sellers, we are not suggesting that you take advantage of someone. A motivated seller truly wants and needs to sell their home to eliminate a problem in their personal situation. If you buy a home from a motivated seller, it usually is a win/win situation. You get a home at a good value and the seller gets to wipe their hands clean of a home that has become a drain on them. Our software searches for both homes and condominiums in all price ranges and areas. See the example on the next page of a home with a motivated seller.

A Home Identified by the Motivated Seller Search

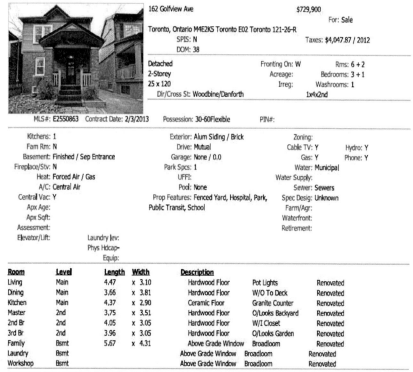

FINDINGS:

In the remarks section, notice that the seller has advertised they are motivated to sell. Often in this scenario there is a specific reason why. If we can provide a suitable solution for the seller we can often work out a good deal on the property. Sometimes it can be as simple as providing a quick closing to relieve financial stress. The goal is to figure out why they are motivated and be the solution.

SEARCH THREE: The Expired Listing Search

An expired listing is a home that was listed for sale with a Realtor for a fixed period of time and didn't sell. Expired listings are really good opportunities because the sellers have already tried to sell their home without any luck.

There are several reasons why homes don't sell. In some cases, the homes are listed in the wrong time of the year. An example would be a nice home that was listed in November or December right before all of the year-end holidays. The real estate market is very slow during these months. Because the market is slow and not many buyers are looking for homes, the seller's home expires without selling.

Just because the seller's home expired without a sale doesn't necessarily mean that they don't want to sell their home. In most cases, they still want to sell their home, but don't know what to do next. They have just been through a rough time on the market. They have been trying to keep their homes clean for months for showings. They have been inconvenienced in their lifestyle with buyers walking through on the evenings and weekends. They have invested all of this time and effort without any sale.

The best part about looking at expired listings when buying a home is you probably will not have any other buyers competing for the home. An expired listing isn't technically on the market, but the sellers usually do want to sell. Because the home isn't technically listed, no other buyers are even considering the home, which leaves it wide open for you. Without any other buyers competing for the home, you can do a much better job negotiating the price to a point that offers you real value.

Our software system will search for homes that expire from their listing contracts. This search occurs daily and all cross-matched homes are automatically sent to you. This search includes both single-family homes and condominiums listed for sale by all of the Realtors in every real estate company.

Here is an example of an expired listing.

A Home Identified by the Expired Listing Search

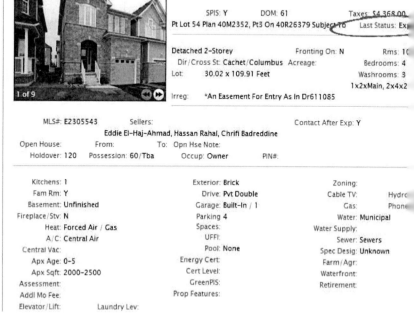

FINDINGS:

In the top right corner of this example, look for the section that has this text: (Last Status: Exp). This means that this home has expired from its listing contract. This four bedroom three bath home, which offers between 2,000 and 2,500 square feet, is no longer listed. However, it is owned by a family that would like to sell it. The sellers would probably entertain a lower offer at this point because of the expired situation.

SEARCH FOUR: The Hot New Listings Search

Understand that I don't recommend this search for our investors because it puts you in competition with other buyers. However, it can be helpful in some situations. You could probably imagine that the homes in nice condition with attractive asking prices sell very quickly. When I say quickly, I mean within days and sometimes within hours. Recently, a listing nearby sold in just four days. In this short period of time, the seller received four separate offers from different buyers.

If you are looking for a specific home, at a specific price, you need to receive very quick information, almost instant details on these homes when they hit the market. If you wait until the weekend newspaper to see what is new, you probably have already missed some great homes because they have already sold. It even gets worse if you wait to find homes advertised in homebuyer guides, like the Harmon Homes and the Homes Almanac. Homes in these booklets have been on the market for at least two weeks because of the lag time needed to print and distribute the books. By the time you pick up a copy, the best homes have already been sold.

This search is performed every minute of every day to find homes that match the home buying criteria we program for you. The search includes:

All Property Styles: Single-family, condominium, multi-family, land, and new construction

All Areas: All of local areas specified

All Price Ranges: All price ranges you specify

All Listings: All listings by all Realtors

All Real Estate Companies: Homes listed by all real estate companies

Once the system identifies a match to your home-buying criteria, we will notify you.

See the next page for an example of a new listing.

Home Identified by the Hot New Listings Home Search

FINDINGS:

In the center of this example, look for the section that has this text: (DOM: 1). This means it has only been on the market for a day. It is a new listing of a three plus two bedroom, two bathroom home. This home offers a fully-finished basement with a couple of bedrooms which means it may be able to be rented as two separate units. There would be a bit of fact checking to do around the ability to rent the property but it will probably sell very quickly if everything is in order. This is why we have to be on top of it so we get ahead of any potential competition.

Now for a strictly Canadian perspective...

When investing, finding the right property can be extremely time consuming usually much more so than many beginners realize.

That is why having a system that will continue to search for the types of properties that make good investments is key. This allows you to stop spending such an incredible amount of time searching for the deal.

Many of our clients in the Greater Toronto Area work full time. Taking into account your daily job, hours spent with friends and family, and taking time for yourself; schedules can fill up quickly. This is where the search system will greatly help them. They can more readily locate a good investment and move forward to start generating profit from it instead of consistently evaluating properties that don't match their criteria.

Too often someone will lose their motivation to invest after running in circles trying to evaluate any property they come across, with a real idea of what they are looking for. There is one client specifically that comes to mind. He told me that before he started working with us he used to visit open houses to get an idea of what was available. He always left empty handed as he had no clear sense of direction.

I had two main concerns:

1. He was looking at any type of house without any sense at all at what he was going to do with it. Different investments work best with specific types of homes.

2. How many homes can you realistically look at when you are going to see open houses? Not many.

Instead of using a system that could search through hundreds or thousand of properties to find matches better suited for his investments he was visiting only a few homes. This is an easy way to get discouraged.

And that is what happened. He told me that he used to leave with a sense of frustration. He knew real estate investing was something he wanted but was having trouble taking that next step.

After using the systems discussed here I am happy to report that at that time of this writing he has two investment properties and is looking at purchasing his third in a few months. He has been able to successfully move forward.

You can leverage what is available to you to overcome similar obstacles. The information is out there but you need a system to do the filtering for you.

9

How To Negotiate Thousands Off Of The Price When You Buy A Home

When making a real estate investment, it is important for you to understand that you make a great deal of money by buying the home below value. If you overpay for a property, it eats at your overall return on investment. You should work hard at becoming a good negotiator because it can literally save you thousands of dollars on each property you buy. For example, negotiating an extra 4% off of a $200,000 home amounts to $8,000 in savings. You are probably asking, how much can you save on a home? And the answer is, *"It depends on the seller of the home you are interested in buying."* Your focus when buying a home is to get the seller below their break point. Understand that every seller has a different break point, depending on his or her situation. When I say break point, I mean the lowest price a seller thought they would accept. So if that is your goal, how do you do it?

You Need to Get Information on the seller's Situation

When one of our clients finds a home that might be a good investment, our whole focus is to get information about the seller and their personal situation. The more information you have about the seller's situation, the more you will negotiate off the price of the home. To give you a real life example of what I mean, consider this home purchase of one of our clients:

Having More Information Saves an Investor $5,500

A few years ago, I was working with some clients looking for a property. We walked through a beautiful colonial that met all of their criteria. Lucky for us, the seller was home during our walk through. Mr. Seller was doing something outside when I just happened to ask, "So why are you selling?" He gave the proper answer for a seller, which was, "We are just moving closer to work." Can you see how his answer didn't give us any information or show any motivation on the seller's part? For a seller, he handled the question perfectly. A few minutes later, we bumped into Mrs. Seller in the kitchen and guess what, I just happened to ask Mrs. Seller, "So why are you selling?" Mrs. Seller proceeded to tell us that they just inherited a large sum of money and they were building a larger new home just a few miles away.

JACKPOT! We hit pay dirt!!

We then structured our offer on this home about 5% below what we normally would have offered on the initial offer. We held firm in our negotiations. The process took a few days, but my clients bought this home for about $4,000 less than they were willing to pay for the home. In this transaction, the seller was asking $99,900. My clients' initial offer was for $88,000. This home was worth around $97,500 because it had a new kitchen, new windows, deck and many other improvements. Typically, the initial offer in this scenario would have been around $92,000 to $93,000. My clients purchased the home for $92,000. In essence, when title transferred into my client's name, their net worth increased by $5,500 (value of $97,500 less price of $92,000). Can you see how having information on the seller's situation can save you thousands of dollars? In reality, one simple question saved these clients thousands of dollars. It's a great question, "So, why are you selling?" Ask it as many times as you can to as many people as you can It will pay off!

It gets even better...

This transaction actually got even better. This colonial had frame (wood) siding that needed to be scraped and painted. My clients had planned on having the home vinyl sided after their purchase. We found out that the city had given the seller a violation to have the home scraped and painted. The seller never disclosed this housing code violation to us, which they are *required to do by law*. We contacted the seller regarding the painting housing code violation and their failure to disclose this item. The seller responded that he had dropped the price of the home to cover the painting costs. However, because he didn't disclose the housing code violation, he was potentially liable for damages. Guess what? To prevent a lawsuit, the seller gave my clients an additional $2,000 to have the home painted. Understand that my clients had already planned on having the house sided anyhow. So this was a big savings to them. In essence, my client bought the home $5,500 under value and then got paid $2,000 for doing it.

SUCCESSFUL NEGOTIATION REALLY COMES DOWN TO THREE KEYS:

1. TIMING
2. INFORMATION
3. STRATEGY

TIMING

In any negotiation you are involved in, try to find out the
sellers' deadline for the completion of sale. When do they
need to sell to prevent a financial nightmare from occurring?
If you can find out the seller's true deadline, then you can use
this deadline to your advantage in your offer. Here is what I
mean. In most cases, the seller of the home you are thinking of
buying has to buy another home. When they close on their
new home, they need a down payment, closing costs and are
now on the hook for two mortgage payments–one payment on
their old home and another payment on their new home. For
most people, this is a costly and scary position to be in. Here is
how you can benefit:

*If you knew that your seller was closing on their new home on
January 15, you can make a lower price offer on the home they
are selling with a closing date before their deadline of January
15.*

The seller would probably be more inclined to lower their price
because it will save them in extra loan fees and the financial
stress of having two house payments at the same time. The
focus here is to use the seller's deadline to your advantage.
Structure your agreement to benefit the seller's deadline at a
lower price for you.

INFORMATION

The more information you have about the seller's situation, the
better prepared you will be. In the above transaction, we knew
the seller's reason for selling. We knew their deadline on
building their new home and we had information of housing

code violations. We used this information to our advantage. Here are some other items that we investigate to give us more information during a negotiation. We search the public records to see when the seller bought the home and for how much. If the seller bought the home within the last year or two at a substantially lower price, they might be more flexible on their current sale price. In most cases, however, what the seller paid for the home has no real bearing on what today's true market value is. We search to see if the seller is current on their property taxes. If the taxes are delinquent, we now know the seller is in need of money fast. So we offer to close very quickly with a lower price, of course. We also search to see if the seller owns any other property. Our focus here is to see if the seller already bought another home. If they own two homes, they are probably making two mortgage payments and are desperate to stop the financial stress. When you find out information on the seller's situation, ask yourself, how can I use this information to my advantage?

STRATEGY (Where the Real Fun Is)

Your strategy is extremely important. Here is just one of the strategies we like to use when we negotiate for our clients. We always ask for stuff that our investor clients don't want. I just chuckled to myself over a past negotiation. A while ago I was meeting with an investor client to prepare an offer for a home. I suggested to my clients that they ask for the seller's piano in the offer. My client got a little irritated with me because he would potentially have to have the piano moved out if his tenant didn't want it. When he finally understood my strategy, he gave me a high five. The seller had no intention of including the piano with the sale. In fact the piano was very dear to them. When we offered the seller a lower price for the home and asked the seller to include the piano in the sale, they got a little upset. The sellers got emotional over the piano request and made a counter offer to my clients, which focused on them keeping the piano. My clients finally agreed to let the seller keep their cherished piano, but held firm on their lower price. Low and behold, they got the home at the lower price and the seller got to keep their cherished piano. You see when you ask for things that you don't want, you can negotiate those items away instead of increasing your price. In this transaction the seller became focused on the piano and lost sight of their price. We focused on the price and lost sight of the piano. Asking for extra items in the offer to buy the home shifts the seller's focus from the price to the other items you ask for.

Combine the Timing and Extra Stuff Strategy

To make this scenario even better, use the seller's deadline with the extra stuff request. In the above example of the seller needing to sell by January 15, offer the seller a closing date of February 15 and also ask for the piano. During the negotiations, the seller will be concerned with two items that you don't even care about. Their deadline of January 15 and the thought of losing their cherished piano. You, of course, would be willing to move up the closing date to before January 15 and let the seller keep the piano, if the seller met your lower price.

Strong negotiating strategy can honestly save you thousands of dollars. Because it is so important, it is one of the key trainings topics for our team members. Consider buying and reading a few good books on negotiations. They can help you with any purchase. The bigger the purchase, the more you can potentially save. Another quick point about buying real estate and using a Realtor to help you:

This is what we do, in fact. We help investors find homes and negotiate the purchase for them. If you are going to invest without help, realize that you need to understand clearly that the Listing Realtor doesn't represent you. A Realtor can either represent a buyer or a seller. In some cases, they can actually work with both the Buyer and the seller together. If a Realtor has a sign in the front yard, they represent the seller. This means that they are required by law to negotiate the highest price and best terms in favor of the seller and not you. Don't be fooled into thinking that the listing Realtor is going to help you get a good deal. If you are going to work with a Realtor to help you find and buy investment properties, make sure he or she is working as a Buyer's Agent. If they are working as a Buyer's Agent, they should be working to get the best price and terms for you, rather than the seller. Also look for an experienced Realtor that has a successful track recorded of strong negotiating skills. In Lake County, Ohio the average Realtor negotiates only about 3.6% off the seller's asking price. Using the strategies discussed in this report and a few others, our team has negotiated an average of 7.7% off of the price for our investor clients. On average, we negotiate 4.1% more off of the price when compared to other Realtors.

Real Life Negotiating Success Story

"I wanted to thank Rob Minton for helping me buy a home substantially below value. I purchased a home for $78,000. Included with the purchase price, the seller paid $2,000 toward my buyer closing costs and $7,000 in escrow for repairs that I wanted to make in the home after title transfer.

My real price on this home was $69,000 ($78,000 less $7,000 less $2,000). At closing my lender's appraiser appraised the home at $82,000. Using various negotiating strategies, Rob and his team helped me buy this home $13,000 ($82,000 less my true price of $69,000) below value. That's almost 16% below market value!" - David Berrow

Additional Negotiating Pointers on Buying Properties on Your Own…

Don't get emotionally involved with the home. Remember get attached to a successful investing approach, not a property. By not getting emotionally attached to the home, you will have the ability to walk away from it. This will help you get the lowest possible price when you buy a home. In fact, a good Realtor can disguise your motivation from the seller and the Listing agent. They act as a buffer for you. A good negotiator on the seller's side can read your non-verbal communications. You always need to be displaying disinterest in a property. This includes verbally and non-verbally. One true sign of motivation is by watching to see….

Who Calls Whom the Most!

Whoever is making more calls to the other party is the motivated one. You should play disinterested, which means you should not be making many calls to the other party in a negotiation. Don't beat the seller's door down. You should hold back and let the seller come to you. I have witnessed many buyers and Realtors show motivation by continuously calling the other party. Understand that when you are the one calling, you have lost control of the negotiation. So, if you go to see a home that is For Sale By Owner, you should always leave your name and number. Your hope is that the seller will call you back after your showing. If the seller calls you, play hesitant. Say something like "Well, I liked the home, but I don't think I can afford your price!" When you say this, you are telling the seller that you are interested but he has to work to get you to buy the home. After you use this technique, stop talking and let the seller respond. In most cases, the seller will ask you what you price you are willing to pay. Another rule of thumb in negotiating is:

Whoever Says a Number First Loses!

When the seller asks you what price you are willing to pay and you answer $XXXX, you could be leaving money on the table. Never name a price, because the seller may be willing to sell the home to you for less. If the seller asks you what price you would be willing to pay, you should respond, "I am not really sure, what is the best you could do?"

At this point, the seller will say a price lower than what they are asking. You should than say something like, "If I could close and transfer title quickly, could you go any lower?" If they ask you how much you are thinking, say, "I am just trying to figure out a way to be able to afford your home. Are there any other options?" Notice that you still haven't named a price. If they offer you a lower price with this technique, tell them that you need to think it over and that you will get back to them.

Now, wait again for seller to call you. Remember, you are working with a motivated seller who has been on the market for a long time. Your patience will be rewarded. If the seller calls you, you got it! At this point, you could say, "Over the weekend, we walked through another home that seems to be a better value. I might be able to swing your home if you could sell it for $XXXXXX." Obviously, your price will be lower than what the seller has already committed to in your earlier discussions. The only time I ever recommend giving the price is when you have the seller at their break point. At this point, I name the price and see if we have a deal.

Another benefit of this technique is that you don't have to low-ball the seller on price. Because you aren't naming a price until the absolute end of the negotiation, you don't run the risk of upsetting them with a low offer. Also, by dragging out the negotiation, you are getting the seller to invest more time into you, plus they may be getting closer to their deadline. Most people don't like to waste their time, so they will work harder to be rewarded for their efforts.

Now for a strictly Canadian perspective...

Those universal negotiating points are excellent and work extremely well in practice. Let me share a few additional points.

Higher Authority

Many people don't use the concept of a "higher authority". I first read about this in '*The Secrets to Power Negotiating*' by Roger Dawson and it works extremely well.

Whenever I negotiate the price of a home (or anything for that matter), I always mention that I will have to run this by another group of people that make the ultimate the decision.

This could be your family or in business, it could be a group of partners. I purposely never mention any specific person so that it's impossible for the person I'm negotiating with to ask to speak with that person directly. I always refer to my "higher authority" as some vague group of people.

By doing this I can negotiate for the best possible price and then take that price away for final approval by my family or my business partners. This gives me the opportunity to come back again and ask for a lower price or some sort of concession "because my business partners are demanding it". It really works well.

Agree First

Next, I often see people get into heated disagreements over a specific topic during the negotiation process.

This tends to alienate both parties from each other and dramatically decreases the chances of an agreement being made. Instead of disagreeing with someone when they challenge me I often agree with them first and then move on to make my case – even if that means I go on to completely disagree with them. I find that by agreeing with them first they lose the will to fight and their defenses go down.

Recently I was renting out an investment property when a lady really got in my face about the monthly rental amount I was asking for. She said it was ludicrous and that I would never be able to get that in this part of the city.

I knew the price I was asking for was fair but instead of just yelling back at her that she was crazy and causing a scene in front of the other possible tenants I had in the house I simply agreed with her.

I said, "Yeah, prices are crazy these days aren't they. I agree. But I don't know what to do. My costs to carry the home are pretty high because of the prices of these homes. If I don't ask for $1,650 per month for this home I can't make this work. It just won't make any business sense to do it. It's really an insane world these days isn't it?"

Now I've done a couple of things here. I've agreed with her that the price is high, so that now she can't argue with me. Her point had been taken, and we are now on the same page. Then I've gone on to explain that the price really has to be this high and I've given her a reason. I've found that once people know your reasons for doing things they are more often willing to accept your price.

In this particular case the lady went on to apply for the home but I didn't select her. Someone else applied who offered me even more than what I was asking for. It's an insane world!

You can use this same strategy when buying an investment property. Here's how it works. When you give a low price on a home be prepared to list of the reasons why you are doing so. And then take it one step further. When you are presenting your offer bring up their objection and agree with it. "Hi Mr. Seller, the price I'm offering is X and I know you think this may be crazy. I can agree that you would think this way. I really can. Here's where I'm coming from…." And go on to list your reason for offering the price.

You have already agreed with the seller in advance that the price is lower than they expected and you agree with them that that it is low. This simply strategy really calms them down and you are left to negotiate with them instead of having to deal with their emotions. When a seller gets emotional in front of you almost nothing you can say will bring the situation to any form of agreement.

So the next time someone disagrees with what you are saying try this out:

1. Agree with them. Explain how you can see things from their point of view.
2. Move on and present your case.

Their will to argue with you will be dramatically reduced.

"You can't get that!"

Finally, another great strategy for getting what you want in a negotiation is to JUST ASK FOR IT.

When I began investing in residential real estate in Ontario we never asked the Seller to pay for our closing costs. These costs included the legal fees, land transfer tax, home inspection and smaller miscellaneous fees.

I was told that this wasn't possible in Canada; it was a U.S. thing that just wasn't done here. I spoke about it at length with some professionals and couldn't find any good reasons for it. So we had our lawyer draft up a clause for it and began asking the Seller to pay for our closing costs. This usually amounted to several thousand dollars. As an investor it was a big deal.

Then we just started asking for it. We just went out and starting including it in our offers. And guess what? After being yelled at for 10 minutes by the seller's agent we ultimately got it done. We were told that this doesn't work in Canada, or it's not legal, or it wasn't right. But every time we pressed for more details no one had any really good reason that we couldn't ask for it. Other agents and sellers were scared of it because it was something new. Confused minds say 'no'. Once we explained what we were asking for we got it.

Now I've seen it used dozens of times and have even heard of other real estate agents using similar clauses. I'm not certain but we may be the very first in Canada to start doing this.

Here's another "just ask for it" story.

When we started doing rent to own programs here in Canada I had friends, family, real estate agents and mortgage brokers all tell me that it wouldn't work. The common theme in their argument was, "Who in their right mind will give you thousands of dollars upfront and then also give you first and last month's rent" or "It may work in the U.S. but that can't work here, Canadians are different".

At the time interest rates were (and still are) historically low and mortgages seemed to be handed out to anyone who could fog a mirror.

Thankfully we completely ignored this advice and went ahead with our plans (*by the way, I've come to realize that when everyone tells me something can't be done I'm likely onto something really big!*). We put up our yard sign and began asking for thousands of dollars upfront plus first and last month's rent.

On that very first home we received $7,500 in nonrefundable deposit money plus first and last month's rent. We walked away with over $10,000 before we even handed the tenant the keys. This all happened before the first mortgage payment was made and we hadn't even made it out to the property for a week and a half after closing due to our busy schedules.

Ask and you shall receive.

One more note on negotiations. I often see first time investors take a hard stance on how much they will pay for a property. They are willing to walk away from a deal because the seller is at his or her break point and will not come down another $1,500.

I find this baffling. Sometimes it's easy to forget that your time is valuable. If you have spent a couple of days or weeks finding a good property and then a few days in negotiation it's not worth it to throw away a good property over $1,500. Your time is valuable.

If you are using a Canadian 10% down investor mortgage program that $1,500 cost you $150 in extra down payment money. And at 6% interest amortized over 40 years that is $8.25 per month in additional carrying costs.

I would like to think that I'm going to make enough money that the extra $8.25 will not put me into a negative cash flow position! And my time is worth much more than $8.25 a month.

I know of an investor who is comfortable with constantly paying 5% over the asking price of homes in his area because he knows how to make money with good homes. It's not worth it to him to lose a home or spend time negotiating. He just goes in with a strong offer and moves on to the next deal. Now that may not be right for everyone but it's interesting to see how he operates.

Look at the big picture and don't get caught up emotionally when negotiating.

10

The Best Way to Market Your Home is to Advertise Three Magic Words "Rent-to-Own"

At this point in the book, you have found a nice home in a nice area and you have used specific negotiating strategies to purchase this home below value. Now you are focused on renting your home to a tenant/buyer on a Rent-to-Own program. Before I go on with a high level approach on this process, let me share with you...

A Big Lesson on Advertising!

I have spent thousands of dollars advertising properties. In the beginning of my real estate sales career, I didn't honestly know what I was doing. I ran advertisements that I thought would make me look good. I finally went out and invested some money to learn about advertising. I hired one of the best real estate agents in the world to coach me. The agent I hired was Craig Proctor. Craig's team sells 400 to 500 homes a year.

You probably don't care much about any of this; however, I learned many incredible lessons from Craig. One of the first lessons that he taught me was regarding advertising. He asked me one day, what is the purpose of advertising? My ignorant response was to promote something I was trying to sell.

Craig's answer to this question literally blew me away. Craig made it very clear that the purpose of advertising was to:

MAKE THE PHONE RING!!!!

The only reason to run any form of advertisement is to make your phone ring. When you write an advertisement, you should try to put yourself in your tenant/buyer's shoes. If you wanted to own your own home today, but didn't qualify for a mortgage, what advertisement would make you want to pick up the phone and make a call? In other words, what benefit does someone get by responding to your advertisement as opposed to any other advertisement in the paper?

Understand that you will not be the only person advertising homes in the paper. You are in essence competing with every other landlord for the tenant/buyers phone call. The landlord with the most calls wins. The landlord with the most calls gets the most qualified tenant! The landlord with the most calls will be able to get their home rented much sooner than a landlord with only a few calls. To put it in the simplest of terms:

THE LANDLORD WITH THE MOST CALLS MAKES THE MOST MONEY!!

In all of my years of marketing investment properties to tenants, I have learned a simple three-step formula. Incorporate the three following points in any advertisement that you prepare.

1. USP, or Unique Selling Proposition
2. Hit Their Emotional Hot Buttons
3. Non-Threatening Way to Get More Information

UNIQUE SELLING PROPOSITION

When I say Unique Selling Proposition, or USP, I simply mean, "Why should someone call you above anyone else?" When you determine this for your property, it should be in the headline. The headline of your advertisement will make or break you. Put your USP in your headline.

HIT THEIR EMOTIONAL HOT BUTTONS

An advertisement should reach out and grab someone emotionally, not logically. You should try to paint a beautiful picture of the home in the advertisement to make someone want to live there.

NON-THREATENING WAY TO GET MORE INFORMATION

Many home buyers and tenants might be interested in your advertisement, but don't want to play phone tag or be hard sold anything. If you can get them to pick up the phone and call you, you should have an automatic salesperson answer the phone and offer compelling benefits of your property to get them more excited. Many landlords make it difficult for someone to get more information on the home. DON'T MAKE THIS SAME MISTAKE! You should have all interested parties call a prerecorded message to get information 24 hours a day, seven days a week.

Here is just one jackpot advertisement that hits all three points of this formula:

SUPER-SIZED RENT TO OWN
Bright Family Sized Eat-In Kitchen. Sparkling Hardwood Floors. Private Fenced in Yard. Lovely home on quiet tree lined street. Credit problems OK.
Free-recorded message with details.
Call 888-845-1234 ID 999.

The Formula Applied:

USP: Rent-to-Own!! With this headline, you are automatically telling the prospective tenant that they can own your home. You are giving them a shot at owning their own home. This is their dream!

Emotional Hot Buttons: Bright Family Sized Eat-In Kitchen. Sparkling Hardwood Floors. Private Fenced in Yard. Lovely Home on Quiet Tree Lined Street. After reading this portion of the advertisement, how did you feel? You should promote emotional items rather than logical items. Don't say Two Bedrooms and One Bath. You're painting a picture with your advertisement. Your picture should be one that the majority of people would be interested in. Also, note that the word *size* was used twice in the advertisement. We already know that the larger homes are more desirable for out tenant/buyers. This should be conveyed in your advertisement.

Non-Threatening Way to Get Information: Free recorded message with details. Anytime we run any form of advertisement, we always include "free recorded message with details." The purpose is to get more people to pick up the phone to call in just to listen. By offering a non-threatening way to get information, you are baby-stepping them into coming to your home. You are telling them that they don't have to speak to anyone when they call.

The best investment you can make if you decide to offer your single-family home on a Rent To Own program is a nice yard sign. Here is the sign that I use, which I highly recommend:

RENT TO OWN
Credit problems OK.
Free recorded message
with Details.
888-845-123

<u>SIX MONEY SAVING ADVERTISING TIPS</u>

1. Invest in a nice quality yard sign. Make your sign generic so that you can use it at any of your homes. My sign is a white background with very bright large red letters. I have found that a nice sign will draw a significant number of calls. If I have a property that will be available, I get my sign out there as fast as possible. My goal is to have the home rented before I have to invest any money in a classified newspaper advertisement. The best part about a

yard sign is that you pay for it only once, but can use it over and over again with future properties!

2. If your home is located on a street without much traffic, consider getting an arrow sign that says, "Rent-to-Own Home Available." Place this arrow sign in an area where there is more drive by traffic to attract more phone calls from your sign. Point the arrow toward your home to get more drive-by traffic.

3. When placing a newspaper advertisement, have your rent–to-own advertisement placed in the "Homes for Rent Section" of the newspaper. I have learned that if you place a rent-to-own advertisement in the "Homes for Sale Section," you will have fewer calls. Remember, the whole goal is to create more demand and more phone calls.

4. These advertisements were designed to generate a high volume of calls. I would prefer to have 100 calls from prospective tenants instead of 10 calls. I stand a better chance of finding a good tenant/buyer when I can choose from 100 prospective tenants rather than just 10. This helps with your screening and ensures a smooth lease and eventual purchase.

5. Test your advertisements on various days of the week. In most cases, running your advertisements on the weekends will provide enough calls for you. However, we have also found that the advertisement pulls strongly during the week. We usually recommend that you run your advertisement every day until you have a tenant/buyer secured! This provides for a continuous and constant flow of prospective tenant/buyers.

6. Don't set individual appointments for every caller. Set a mini open house and leverage your time. I usually have all of them come at the same time. By having many people at one time, I create an auction like environment and force demand for the home. In fact, we recommend using a voicemail system to set up your showing appointments (see below).

VOICEMAIL SYSTEM: AN ABSOLUTE MUST!

When I started investing in rental properties, I always used my personal home number. When I had a home available for rent, the calls came to my personal number. I had calls from 6 in the morning to midnight. Every time we sat down for dinner, we had more calls. If we rented a movie for a quiet night, we had more calls. I began to hate my rental properties because they controlled me. You must do everything you can to prevent rental property burnout. If you get burned out, you will sell your property and chop down the money tree that is adding extra income streams into your life.

You must control your rental properties and your time. It is important for you to treat your rentals as a business and separate yourself as much as possible. The best way to accomplish this is to set up a separate voicemail system. Most systems can page you if necessary. This should be the only number that you ever give your tenants. You should also un-list your personal home number from the phone book and make your home number private so that it doesn't show up on your tenant's caller ID. This is so important that I can't emphasize it enough. Here is just one story on the value of separating yourself personally from your investment properties:

A few years ago when I was providing my personal number to tenants, I had a very ugly experience with a tenant. We inherited this particular deadbeat tenant when we purchased a property. Not only did this tenant not pay the rent that was due, but also made harassing phone calls to my wife while I was at work. We would have calls at three in the morning. The list goes on. When I was at work, I was worried for the welfare of my family. Have you ever received an obscene phone call at three in the morning without being able to go back to sleep for the remainder of the night?

In addition to a separate voicemail, you should get a separate Post Office box for your rent payments. You really don't want tenants knowing where you live. Prevent any potential ugliness by setting the basics up in the beginning. The voicemail and Post Office box can be paid from the positive cash flow of your properties and both are tax-deductible investing expenses.

When you have a home available for rent, consider these points:

➢ Offer a pre-recorded message with details of the home and Rent To Own program. This gives people 24/7 access to information. By providing a pre-recorded message (see attached script), you can automatically set up showing appointments without having to make one phone call. Over the years, I have spent hundreds of hours calling prospective tenants to set up a time to show them the home. In many cases, I would get their voicemails and would have to play phone tag with them for the showing appointment. Use your voicemail to provide the directions, date and time of your showing to save you time returning phone calls. I actually prefer that the callers drive by the home before I waste any time talking with them. By giving the property address and directions in the voicemail script, I ensure that the prospective tenants will drive by the home. A prospective tenant that has driven by the home is a very good prospect. They already like the home, street and neighborhood.

➢ The pre-recorded message is like a sales robot that you have that works perfectly each and every time. If you are having a bad day, you won't lose a great tenant/buyer by handling the call wrong. Your pre-recorded script works automatically each and every time. This significantly leverages your time.

Quick Tip: The voicemail system that I use is a toll-free hotline system that offers 5 different mailboxes. This means that you can be marketing 5 different properties at the same time. In addition, a tenant/buyer can request and receive a fax automatically from the system. You could have a feature sheet providing room sizes, a map and dates and times of your showings faxed directly to them to potentially pre-screen the tenant further. All this could happen while you are sleeping! Another nice feature with the system is that it can automatically email you with all messages. The fees for the system are $9.95 per month and you can find more information on this system at
http://www.fvsystems.com/09165

Sample Rent-to-Own Voicemail Script

Hello and thank you for calling about this beautiful rent-to-own home. Our Rent-to-Own program offers you the opportunity to quickly and easily move into your own home right now. You don't have to qualify with any banks, or have perfect credit for this program. We even have a program for you to earn your down payment.

This lovely home is located at _____ (*Give the actual street address and directions to the home*). This_____ (*Give emotional appealing information on your home. Example: This spacious four fbedroom colonial offers one and half baths, sparkling hardwood floors, a beautiful remodeled kitchen, a bright formal dining room, a gas fireplace, central air conditioning for those hot summer months and a full basement plus a two-car garage.*)

We will be showing this home on _____(*Specific Day, Date and Time*). We will only be at this home until _____(*End Time of Showing*). If you're planning on stopping by at this time, please leave your name and phone number at the tone. It's important that you leave your name and phone number at the tone, so that if we need to cancel this showing time we can call you to reschedule.

If you aren't able to attend this showing, please leave your name and both a day and evening phone number. If the home isn't sold with our special Rent-to-Own program on _____ (*Showing Day, Date and Time*), we can call you with our next showing date and time.

So, once again, please leave a message with your name, day and evening phone numbers, and also let us know if you plan

to attend the home showing at _____(*Property Address*)
On _____ (*Day, Date and Time*)

Thanks for calling and here comes the tone!

VOICEMAIL SCRIPT NOTES

NOTE 1: I have not included the buyout price in the script. Obviously you will be setting your buyout price at the ESTIMATED FUTURE MARKET VALUE. You don't want to turn a tenant/buyer off on the buyout price before they have even had a chance to see the home. Typically, buyers/tenants change their outlook on a property once they have a chance to walk through and start mentally picturing themselves living in the home.

NOTE 2: I am not trying to explain the Rent-to-Own program in the voicemail script. I do include emotional appeal by telling a little bit more about the home. The goal of the voicemail script is to get as many callers to stop at the home's showing.

NOTE 3: Make sure you remember to change the voicemail script right after a showing. If you don't record a new script with a new showing date and time, you will have to manually call everyone who leaves a message after the recorded showing date and time. Spend the five minutes to record the new script; it will save you an hour of phone calls.

Now for a strictly Canadian perspective...

There are huge money making lessons for you in this chapter.

On my first rental property, I got so discouraged by having to drive to my rental property every time someone wanted to see it that I almost gave up.

At the time, I lived in Mississauga, Ontario and the house was about a 30 minute drive away. I would get calls at all hours and then scramble to make myself available. This would often involve racing home from the grocery store, dropping off my wife and son, throwing the groceries into the house and then racing down to the property to meet the possible tenant.

I was letting the possible tenant control me! I just agreed to whatever time they wanted. I wanted to rent out the house and was willing to do anything to get it done. I thought I was doing the right thing.

When I arrived at the property the possible tenant stayed in control. They would point out everything that was wrong with the property and then tell me I was asking too much for it. It was a complete nightmare.

On the drive home I would call my wife and tell her that I didn't get them to sign a lease and the house would be vacant for another night at least. Not fun.

After a couple of weeks of taking phone calls while I was in the frozen goods section of Loblaws and then pretending I was a NASCAR race car driver on the highway I decide enough was enough.

I decided to have everyone come to the house at the same time. We just told everyone that we would be there on Saturday at 2pm and they could take it or leave it. I didn't care anymore.

I'll never forget that Saturday. We made it down to the house 30 minutes early, cleaned up a little and then at exactly 2pm hoards of people ended up on the front lawn.

We had at least 40 people standing on the front lawn wanting to get into the house. We had one person doing the tours, my brother-in-law was the door man and I managed the line up outside by giving everyone a number that indicated their turn to tour the house.

Suddenly no one cared that there was a tiny rip in the carpet or that one of the doors didn't close smoothly. We had accidentally created a hungry and competitive market for our product (the house). It was fantastic! We were back in control. Forty five minutes later we had signed leases and cold hard cash. What a huge 'ah-hah' moment.

From that point on we have never gone back to the old way of renting out homes.

And now, we use 24 hour voice mail boxes to share details of the home and set appointments.

That way I don't have to worry about dropping one of my kids into the frozen food section of the grocery store while I'm holding my cell phone trying to convince someone to meet me at the house at 6pm instead of 9pm.

We now mention that we require upfront deposits for all our houses and put that in the voice mail message as well. That way we don't have to surprise anyone with this detail when they are at the house talking to us.

It's amazing what you can accomplish by systemizing the process instead of being reactive to it.

I've found that by using small classified ads, yard signs and the 24 hour message system, I can fill a home in a few weeks without many hassles.

We have now tweaked the process even further by using special sign in sheets and managing the way we describe the rent to own programs. Looking back to those first few experiences it's almost embarrassing how silly I had behaved.

Systemize your investing for maximum results.

11

How to Show Your Home to Rent-to-Own Tenants

Step One: Set the Appointment and Don't Do Anything Else
When setting your showing appointments with your prospective tenants, don't give them any information over the phone. I have learned that you can't sell the home over the phone. I have also learned that the prospective tenants will have trouble trying to understand your program without seeing it on paper. If they ask you questions about the program, just say, "I don't have time right now; would it be OK if I answer your questions when we see each other at the home?" Don't spend too much time on the phone with each caller. Just set the appointment and move on! You might want to tell them a few of the nice things about the home to help them stay excited about it!

Step Two: Prepare Your Home for the Showing
Your goal in preparing your home for showings is to make it feel bigger and brighter. Make sure that you open all of the drapes and get as much sunlight as possible into the home. If your home is vacant, take a few lights with you. Some of my properties don't have ceiling lights, so I have to take standing lamps to illuminate the rooms. Turn all of the lights on in the home to make it even brighter. If there are any ceiling fans, turn them on so that your prospective tenants notice them. If it's hot outside, turn on the air conditioning and make the home

feel cool. If you have a fireplace, have a nice fire lit. Have some plug in air fresheners! Set the stage for your home!

Step Three: Create an Auction-Like Environment
Remember I suggested that you schedule all of your showings at the same time? The reason for this is two-fold. One reason is that a group showing saves you a tremendous amount of time in showing the home to each caller individually. Another reason is that it creates immediate demand for your home. When a prospective tenant gets to your home and sees 15 other people looking at your home, human nature kicks in. They automatically don't want to lose the home. You literally will have them competing with each other.

Step Four: Have Them Sign In
Have them sign in on a sign in sheet. This will be helpful for you to track who attended the showing versus those that didn't show. If you didn't get a strong tenant, you can then go back and call the people who didn't show first, before you have to spend additional funds on another advertisement. There will always be people who aren't available during your scheduled times. You might find it necessary to have another open house.

Step Five: Don't Show the Home
When they come to the door, introduce yourself and ask them to sign in. Tell them that they can feel free to walk through the home. Let them know that you can answer any questions that they might have when they are finished with their tour. Understand that some people will walk through and just leave. This is fine with me. I would rather not invest time in talking with them if they don't like the home. If they are interested, they will come back to you. Answer their questions and

explain your program. Give them a rental application to complete.

Step Six: The Rental Application
Tell them that if they are interested, they need to complete the rental application now. Don't give them a chance to fax it, mail it, or drop it off. If you give them an opportunity to take it with them, they will. Trust me from experience; if they take the application, you will never see them again. Explain to them that you have a lot of people who are interested and that you will be making a decision within the next day or so. With the group showings, they will already know this! If they aren't able to complete the application now, they won't be considered for the home. Let them fill out the application. I charge a $20.00 application fee. I have found that this screens out poor quality tenants. If they are in rough financial shape, they won't want to give $20 because they can guess that they won't be selected.

Step Seven: The Quick Check and THEIR UP-FRONT DOWN PAYMENT
When they hand you their application, review their driver's license with the information that they have presented on the application. Tell them that your goal in selecting tenants is to select the applicant that you feel would take the best care of the home during the lease period and also be the most serious about buying the home through the program. Explain to them that your experience has taught you that the tenant who is able to put the most amount of money down up front usually turns out to be the best tenant. After you have explained this to the applicant, ask them again how much money they have to put down on the home. Show them how this money will be subtracted from the final sales price when they buy the home.

Make it clear to them that there are many other applicants for the home and the amount of money that they have available to put down is a big factor in your selection process.

Quick Tip#1: Once in a while, a tenant will ask if they get their up-front payment back if they don't buy the home. I say, "No, your up-front payment isn't refundable. If I select you for the home and invest two years into helping you buy the home and you decide not to buy, the up-front payment stays with me as compensation for taking my home off of the market. If you're not 100% committed to owning this home, we shouldn't even talk anymore about it." This response does two things: 1) Lets them know that you are very serious about them buying the home. 2) You are doing the walk-away close with them. You are taking their dream away from them. You will seem to be disinterested in them. When you use this approach, they will shift gears and be very anxious to take the next step. This walk-away close works perfectly every time I use it!

Quick Tip #2: Many times a prospective tenant will ask you how much they need to move in. In the past, I used to say, "A thousand dollars plus the first month's rent." By responding this way, I lost a lot of money. The correct response is, "How much do you have available?" When you set the amount, it may be well below what they were willing to pay. Try to let them set the amount. Once they set the amount, ask for more money down. See Step Nine for how to do this.

Step Eight: Screen the Applications and Check Their Credit

Call and check the references listed in the rental applications.
We provide our clients with step-by-step instructions on what
to do to evaluate a prospective rental application. Check the
applications and decide on the best candidate very quickly.
Tenants do not wait around. If you are very busy, call them
back and tell them you have ranked them the highest at this
point and let them know that you will be getting back to them
soon. By using this trick, you stop them from looking at other
homes. I have lost countless tenants by being to slow on
checking the applications and getting back to them. TIMING
IS CRUCIAL!

Step Nine: Play the I-Have-Someone-Else Game

Always make your applicants feel like you have a ton of
applications to review. If they feel that they are the only one,
they will control the process. If they feel like they could lose
the home to someone else, you will control the process. Here
is what I mean: Let's say that you narrow it down to the best-
qualified tenant. You can call them and say, "It's between you
and another family. I really think that you're the best fit for the
home; however, the other family is putting more money down.
Is there any chance that you could increase the amount down?"
If they don't think you have anyone else, you will never be
able to get them to increase their up-front payment on the
home. One of the biggest mistakes I see new investors make is
becoming eager to rent to a tenant. If you are ever eager to
rent to a tenant, don't show it! Always make it seem like you
have someone else ready to sign the contract.

Quick Tip: Always ask for more money down. If they told you that they had $2,500, ask if there is any way they could come up with $3,000. Once you ask the question, stop talking! Let them respond. If they are at their absolute maximum available, try this approach: "I would really like for you to have the home, but the other family is offering more money down. Is there any chance that you might be able to pay a little extra for the first few months toward the up-front payment?" Once again, stop talking after you ask the question. In most cases, the tenant would be able to make installment payments to you over time. Work out a mutually agreeable amount and schedule a time to meet them! Taking extra money in installments is a technique that could easily put an extra $1,000 in your pocket from each home. Try it. It works!

Step Ten: Set an Appointment to Sign Their Papers
Once you have negotiated to have them give a higher up-front payment, congratulate the tenant and tell them that it's their home. Schedule a time as soon as possible to meet with them to do the paperwork. Don't delay in meeting with them. Read the chapter on investing mistakes. It could save you thousands of dollars!

Now for a strictly Canadian perspective...

Following the basics is important and listening to the lessons in this chapter is also. It will help you generate more income from your investment.

We hold a personal record of having a home rented out in forty five minutes, using many of these principles. As discussed in the previous chapter we accidentally implemented them without even knowing the difference they would make or exactly what is was we were doing. But after our success we circled back to look at exactly how we did it.

And that's when we realized that in that 45 minute trip we had signed lease agreements worth $27,600! Not bad for the time invested.

We work with our clients to carefully explain this system and the other lessons we have learned throughout our years investing. We feel it is important to empower others so we train our clients to use this system most effectively at no charge.

Another very important lesson is to keep the momentum going with your potential tenant/buyers. It is a great feeling when someone has expressed their interest and verbally committed to moving into your home. But until you actually have cold hard cash in your hands you must keep moving forward quickly or you run a serious risk of losing them.

Make sure you control the situation and set next steps at the time they fill out the application. You never know what can change in a short period of time.

Your potential clients should be called back within 24 hours to get the process started. Keep them excited and get them moving towards the end of the process, signing the agreements. Stay focused and don't halt the things that you have in motion.

Things to remember:

1. Keep your advertising going until the whole process is completed. If the process gets completed you have more leads to work with for your next investment it is only a positive, and one that will work to your advantage.

2. Follow-up with outstanding leads. Don't just collect them. Leads can get cold quick! Sometimes people need a place in a week and have to move. Don't make the mistake of letting them sit before you have signed lease agreements and have money in hand.

3. Keep showing the property. Don't brush people aside, they may be future tenant/buyers that you can place into another investment. Allowing them to meet you and see the types of nice homes you invest in is a huge form of leverage. It can be used as a relationship starter to give them a level of comfort to work with you. Many of our clients have used our lessons to get interested people from one of their houses into their next investment. This greatly reduces their investment risks. It can do the same for you!

The lessons in this chapter are extremely important. They can make you tens of thousands of dollars in a few days.

How long does it take you to make that now?

12

How You Can Make $48,321 on One Single-Family Home in Your Spare Time...

In this chapter, we will take an all Canadian look at some of the homes that our members have invested in and the results for their efforts. The examples are the results of applying an investing approach that has been refined, perfected, and proven for over a decade. Now that approach has become international through the *Income for Life* membership (IFL). Income for Life is a group of highly trained Wealth Coaches who educate and guide investors on how to make money successfully at real estate investing. As you will see, **many of the members make more money in their spare time investing than they do at their nine to five jobs.** Income for Life focuses its investing approach to real estate on a simple rent-to-own strategy. It's a SYSTEM built for buying and profiting from single-family homes. *This SYSTEM actually puts your rental property on autopilot and locks in substantial profits.*

Let's face it; the real money in real estate is the profit between what you pay for a property and what you sell it for.

Income for Life members invest in a property and within weeks have a buyer signed up to purchase their investment at a substantially higher price.

They are able to achieve this by creating enormous demand for their investment properties. They are able to have tenant/buyers compete for their homes, which increases their financial returns. We help our members identify the best properties for investment. In addition, we design and help them implement a program that attracts hungry tenant/buyers by the droves. We show our members how to make these hungry tenant/buyers compete for their home.

This chapter outlines actual case studies of investments made by Income for Life members. The best part of helping investors profit from real estate is that we collectively learn from each other because everyone applies our techniques in a slightly different way. The differences are actually incredible. Sometimes the smallest change can provide a major breakthrough which adds to everyone's income. These little hinges swing really big doors!

You can build an income that exceeds your paycheck!

Here is a very serious question to ask: <u>If all you do is buy one or two homes in the next few months and never do anything else, will you be better off?</u>

The following is a summary of 22 investments made by Income for Life Members. In each of these transactions, the investor (our member) did not have to pay for the team's fees. In every property listed below, the seller paid for the team's services out of their sale proceeds. For several of the properties, our members hired us to show and sell the home to their prospective tenant. We negotiated to have the seller pay for this service as well.

For the investments shown, our members have locked in $1,063,066 in gross profits. Many of these properties were located in market areas having average appreciation of 4-6% a year. The majority of the properties didn't require repairs or updating by our members. Within weeks of buying the property, our members had money from their tenant-buyer in their pocket. These same members were then set up to receive an automatic monthly cash flow from their investments until their tenant/buyer closes the sale.

The Average Profit Per Property is $48,321.18

The investments included here are only a small number of those that our members have made. It would take an entire set of encyclopedias to cover all of them. The key for you to understand is that these profits will be made in areas all around where you live and work. Most beginning investors don't believe that they can make $48,321.18 on a home without having to fix, repair or rehab it. This chapter will prove without doubt that it can be done. Our members do it every week without fail!

In fact, your big dreams in life will never happen until you get started.

Income For Life Member: Nenad Momcilovic (IT Professional)

"I'm currently excited to buy more properties. Tom and Nick offered me a sense of security because I knew that I was not alone throughout the process and they were there to help me make the best decisions.
It's a great feeling knowing that you have real estate mentors/coaches who have actually done it and done it so many times that they can identify any pitfalls early in the investing cycle." - Nenad Momcilovic, Oakville ON

Taymall Ave. Hamilton, ON, Canada	
Member Paid for Property:	$ 213,395
Upfront Payment Received from Tenant:	$ 10,000
Positive Monthly Cash Flow:	$ 220
Contract Sale Price to Buyer:	$ 249,000
Total Locked In Profit on Investment:	**$ 38,885**

Nenad collected the cheque below only 7 days after he took possession of the property. This cheque was in addition to the $1,000 he collected two days after he owned the home.

In total he collected $13,100 before he even made a single mortgage payment!

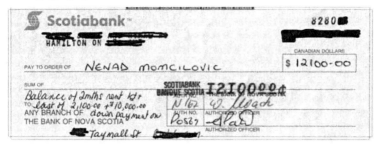

Income For Life Member: Ron Heyden (Robotics Technician)

Taylor Crescent, Burlington, ON, Canada	
Member Paid for Property:	$ 276,000
Upfront Payment Received from Tenant:	$ 3,000
Positive Monthly Cash Flow:	$ 210
Contract Sale Price to Buyer:	$ 324,000
Total Locked In Profit on Investment:	**$ 53,040**

Income For Life Members: Tony & Marilou Soria (Business Professionals)

Sunley Crescent, Brampton, ON, Canada	
Member Paid for Property:	$ 302,000
Upfront Payment Received from Tenant:	$ 13,000
Positive Monthly Cash Flow:	$ 525
Contract Sale Price to Buyer:	$ 363,899
Total Locked In Profit on Investment:	**$ 61,899**

Take note of the monthly cash flow in Tony & Marilou's property. They bring in $525 a month just from the rent being paid. Most investors need to own 3 or 4 homes to get the amount of monthly cash flow but using the Income For Life system they have done it with just one property.

Could you use $525 a month in extra income for owning one property?

Tony & Marilou immigrated from the Philippines and are some of the nicest people we've ever met. Over the years we have known them; they have gone on to build an impressive investment portfolio using these strategies.

Income For Life Member: Jason Jenson (Regional Sales Manager)

Pearson Rd. Brampton, ON, Canada	
Member Paid for Property:	$ 367,000
Upfront Payment Received from Tenant:	$ 7,000
Positive Monthly Cash Flow:	$ 510
Contract Sale Price to Buyer:	$ 436,900
Total Locked In Profit on Investment:	**$ 82,140**

As you can see Jason locked in over $82,000 in just one deal. Jason moved quickly when he started working with us and he now owns 6 properties that make him $3,194 a month in positive cash flow.

That adds up to $38,328 in yearly income. That is more than the average yearly income in the country. Jason has created a full time second income for himself except he doesn't need to work 40 hours a week for the money.

But the best part about this is that Jason was able to accomplish this is only 14 months.

We were so impressed with his achievement that we presented him with a special award at one of our Members Only Private meetings where we all share tips and strategies to our success. This is the picture of the presentation.

Income For Life Member: Jude Dholah (Business Analyst)

Palmer Road, Hamilton, ON, Canada	
Member Paid for Property:	$ 235,000
Upfront Payment Received from Tenant:	$ 5,000
Positive Monthly Cash Flow:	$ 515
Contract Sale Price to Buyer:	$ 262,500
Total Locked In Profit on Investment:	$ 39,860

Jude implemented the most important lesson in investing. He took action. Jude told me that he knew he wanted to invest in real estate and would commonly visit open houses on weekends but didn't know where to go from there. It made him frustrated. But he started working with our team and immediately started generating cash flow and wealth. Here are some of his comments:

> *"This system really does work! It's so helpful to be able to bounce ideas and share strategies with Real Estate coaches who are active investors.*
> *They understand your concerns and are able to walk you through the process because they have done it themselves. I would highly recommend Tom and Nick and their Income for Life program to anyone looking at investing in Real Estate. Thanks guys."*

From the sounds of the first line Jude may have had some lingering doubts but as you can tell from all the examples in this chapter overcoming fear and taking action are profitable.

Income For Life Member: Bill McCarley (Retired)

Heathwood Ct., Cambridge, ON, Canada	
Member Paid for Property:	$ 255,000
Upfront Payment Received from Tenant:	$ 10,000
Positive Monthly Cash Flow:	$ 375
Contract Sale Price to Buyer:	$ 287,500
Total Locked In Profit on Investment:	**$ 41,500**

Bill was retired when he started investing in real estate. He had spent 'thousands' of dollars on different training programs but they didn't give him the 'real life system' that he was looking for. Here is part of an email we received from him.

"Thank you, Well I got 'er done in just 11 days. I collected $1,800.00 cash as a hold deposit and will receive the balance ($8,200.00) plus first month's rent ($1650.00) for a grand total of $11,650.00 which equals 78.43% upfront ROI." - Bill McCarley, Mississauga, ON

Income For Life Member: Kevin Tulk (Technician)

Fieldnest Drive, Whitby, ON, Canada	
Member Paid for Property:	$ 279,000
Upfront Payment Received from Tenant:	$ 10,000
Positive Monthly Cash Flow:	$ 375
Contract Sale Price to Buyer:	$ 319,000
Total Locked In Profit on Investment:	**$ 40,000**

Income For Life Members: Dianna Duffy & Gus Casciaro (Contractor)

Shipley Ave., Newcastle, ON, Canada	
Paid for Property:	$ 244,000
Upfront Payment Received from Tenant:	$ 8,700
Positive Monthly Cash Flow:	$ 447
Contract Sale Price to Buyer:	$ 283,000
Total Locked In Profit on Investment:	**$ 39,540**

Income For Life Member: Todd Gordon (Business Owner)

Peter Street, Burlington, ON, Canada	
Member Paid for Property:	$ 275,000
Upfront Payment Received from Tenant:	$ 5,000
Positive Monthly Cash Flow:	$ 208
Contract Sale Price to Buyer:	$ 325,800
Total Locked In Profit on Investment:	**$ 55,792**

Income For Life Member: Om Sadhana (Factory Worker)

Brampton, ON, Canada	
Member Paid for Property:	$ 260,000
Upfront Payment Received from Tenant:	$ 7,500
Positive Monthly Cash Flow:	$ 115
Contract Sale Price to Buyer:	$ 306,000
Total Locked In Profit on Investment:	**$ 48,760**

The Total Profit from Investment has increased with each investment. The reason why the average profit per property is increasing is because we continually test different approaches and strategies. With each change and adjustment, we learn how to improve our results. We report each new idea and strategy in the monthly Income for Life Members Newsletter. When you are plugged in with this monthly newsletter, you can achieve the same profit increases with your investments. In addition, new Income for Life Members receive our step-by-step Rent-to-Own SYSTEM. This step-by-step guide also includes all of the forms and contracts that we use with our investments.

Income For Life Member: Francis Moon (Financial Planner)

Brucedale Avenue, Hamilton, ON, Canada	
Member Paid for Property:	$197,000
Upfront Payment Received from Tenant:	$ 5,000
Positive Monthly Cash Flow:	$ 350
Contract Sale Price to Buyer:	$223,807
Total Locked In Profit on Investment:	**$ 35,207**

Income For Life Members: Sergio and Vita Podda

Denison Ave., Brampton, ON, Canada	
Member Paid for Property:	$ 299,000
Upfront Payment Received from Tenant:	$ 9,000
Positive Monthly Cash Flow:	$ 650
Contract Sale Price to Buyer:	$ 354,233
Total Locked In Profit on Investment:	**$ 55,233**

Income For Life Member: Mike Desormeaux (Real Estate Sales)

Grindstone Way, Waterdown, On, Canada	
Member Paid for Property:	$ 379,000
Upfront Payment Received from Tenant:	$ 20,000
Positive Monthly Cash Flow:	$ 596
Contract Sale Price to Buyer:	$427,517
Total Locked In Profit on Investment:	$ 62,821

Did you notice anything special about this story? Mike was able to collect **$20,000 as a deposit** on this home. That was an Inner Circle record at the time.

Even better was that Mike collected this money before he committed to the purchase of the property. It was like he was being paid to purchase the property.

Are you interested in collecting $20,000 before you commit to purchasing an investment property?

Income For Life Members: C. & L. Garcia

153rd St. Surrey, BC, Canada	
Member Paid for Property:	$ 253,000
Upfront Payment Received from Tenant:	$ 8,000
Positive Monthly Cash Flow:	$ 550
Contract Sale Price to Buyer:	$ 288,420
Total Locked In Profit on Investment:	$ 48,620

Income For Life Members : Matt & Gino Spada
(Entrepreneurs)

Neils Ave., Burlington, ON, Canada	
Member Paid for Property:	$ 321,000
Upfront Payment Received from Tenant:	$ 10,000
Positive Monthly Cash Flow:	$ 330
Contract Sale Price to Buyer:	$ 368,304
Total Locked In Profit on Investment:	**$ 47,304**

Matt and Gino have had such success that a National Magazine wanted them to share some of the lessons they picked up from their Rock Star Inner Circle membership.

Here is a picture from the magazine article and Gino's thoughts on his experience.

"Making a difference means a lot to me in my life journey. Whether it be something I've done or something I've said. If I can't make a difference, I usually do and say nothing. Once in a while someone makes a difference if my life by something they said or done, and that is why I'm thankful for the day that I met Tom and Nick Karadza. They've made a significant difference in my life." - Gino Spada

Dynamic duo boasts a dozen properties – and still counting

Income For Life Members: Christine & Gord Stanyon

Belleau St. Stoney Creek, ON, Canada	
Member Paid for Property:	$ 268,000
Upfront Payment Received from Tenant:	$ 20,000
Positive Monthly Cash Flow:	$ 58
Contract Sale Price to Buyer:	$ 310,000
Total Locked In Profit on Investment:	**$ 42,000**

This is only one of the homes Christine and her father have invested in. Like many members they have gone on to invest in more. Here is a $19,000 bank draft they were given from the people who moved into the property.

Income for Life Member: Joe & Steve Skrinjar (Contractors)

Birchcliffe Cres. Hamilton, ON, Canada	
Member Paid for Property:	$ 204,000
Upfront Payment Received from Tenant:	$ 5,000
Positive Monthly Cash Flow:	$ 250
Contract Sale Price to Buyer:	$ 252,810
Total Locked In Profit on Investment:	**$ 54,810**

Steve and Joe are brothers that own a construction company. They used to flip properties before joining the Inner Circle. Once they started following our program they couldn't believe that they had spent all that time fixing up old homes. They set a record of investing in four homes in only five weeks!

Income for Life Member: Jon Paul Hunt (Sales Professional)

102 Broken Oak, Cambridge, ON, Canada	
Member Paid for Property:	$ 219,000
Upfront Payment Received from Tenant:	$ 3,000
Positive Monthly Cash Flow:	$ 50
Contract Sale Price to Buyer:	$ 245,000
Total Locked In Profit on Investment:	**$ 27,200**

Jon Paul invested in his first property even before he bought his own home! He was able to invest in this property with absolutely nothing out of his own pocket and STILL get a positive cash flow every month.

He said 'it feels like I am printing money' since he didn't use a single dollar out of his pocket to generate over $27,000 dollars of locked in profits.

Income For Life Member: Wayne Neale (Financial Industry)

Candlebrook Drive, Whitby, ON, Canada	
Member Paid for Property:	$ 254,900
Upfront Payment Received from Tenant:	$ 4,000
Positive Monthly Cash Flow:	$ 350
Contract Sale Price to Buyer:	$148,837
Total Locked In Profit on Investment:	**$ 39,368**

Let's face it, all the money is in taking action. Real estate will continue to make investors wealthy with or without you, as it has already. If you ever want to retire, you better have passive income coming to you each month, or you will be forced to work your entire life!

We are currently working with a new client who has told me that he has been thinking of investing for fifteen years.

Do you know how much he has made from his investment business in those years?

Absolutely nothing.

If you continue to 'think' about it you will never progress. You need to 'do' something, you can't just 'think about it. You need take the next steps and move forward to make something happen. Only then will you increase your wealth year over year in your spare time.

Do something!

Decide What You Want and Take Action Now!

162

13

Investor Mistakes, Foul Ups, and Blunders…

This chapter is a challenging one to prepare because I have to reveal mistakes that I have made as an investor. I have honestly made so many investing mistakes over the last few years that it would make your head spin. Fortunately, I have realized that mistakes are part of the learning process. It seems that now, when something doesn't go quite the way I had hoped, I am able to step back and assess the situation to see where I could have handled something differently. Many people give up when they encounter a failure or make a mistake. Many people also listen to others who have made mistakes and don't learn from these valuable lessons. The biggest thing that I have learned that I can share with you is that:

The lesson you are supposed to learn will be given to you repeatedly until you FINALLY learn it!!!

One of my mentors used to say, *"If you throw a rock up in the air and it comes back to hit you in the head, don't throw the rock up again."* I used to follow this advice; however, now I have learned to throw the rock up again but in a different direction!!! For me it doesn't make any sense not to throw the rock up again. You went through all of the effort to throw the rock the first time. You even had to suffer from the pain of the rock hitting your head. You now have learned a very valuable lesson, which is not to throw the rock up straight over your

163

head. You are farther along than most people with this hard earned lesson. Don't waste this lesson by not trying again. The majority of people give up too quickly. We have a saying in our office that helps us get through challenging times. That saying is *"Quitters never win and winners never quit!"* Winners keep going. They keep moving forward trying new strategies and learning more and more. They use this compounding of experience to their benefit with each new property.

Some of the mistakes detailed within this chapter were our client's mistakes. We have their permission to tell their stories so that you may benefit in some way. These mistakes aren't in any particular order. My hope is that you can learn and not make the same mistakes that we have made in our investing endeavors. In fact, you can take a quantum leap as an investor by learning from other investors' experiences. However, be careful whom you listen to! When you listen to someone's advice, you usually get what he or she has. Unless you want what they have, don't listen to them!

MISTAKE ONE: Feeling sorry for someone and renting to them

I can honestly say that every single time I have felt sorry for a prospective tenant and rented to him or her, I have been burned. I was given this lesson several times during my investing career. Here is the story of how I finally learned this lesson for the last time. We had a nice three bedroom, one and a half bath split-level home for rent under a Rent To Own program a few years ago. It was wintertime around the holidays and I got a call from a man who was staying in a hotel. In fact, his whole family was staying there because their home had just burned down. It really did burn down; he wasn't just feeding me a story. The fire was in the newspapers and my heart went out to him. During this call, he cried and told me how the family dog was lost in the fire. I could just hear the pain in his voice. I couldn't imagine losing everything that I owned. This gentleman was a landscaper, so his income wasn't very stable. Considering his credit score, which wasn't good, and his lack of income, I wouldn't typically rent to this person. However, his homeowner's insurance policy was going to cover the rent to us while his burned down home was rebuilt. Because I felt so bad that his family lost everything, I rented to him. I put the Rent-to-Own program on hold and rented to him under a straight month-to-month rental agreement. His home was supposed to be rebuilt within the next few months, at which point, they would vacate our property and we could launch our Rent to Own program again.

One year later, his home wasn't rebuilt and his insurance company had stopped paying our rent. Eventually, we had to start the eviction process. Luckily, they moved out before we had to go to court, so we didn't have to formally evict this family from our home. Their house was almost rebuilt by this time, so they moved into their unfinished home. That was the good news. The bad news was that they destroyed our home. We had to completely renovate the interior and exterior of the home to a tune of several thousand dollars.

They apparently had many dogs and the flea population was living large in our house. The very first time, I went into the home after they vacated, I had to drive home in my underwear. No I am not some pervert. My clothes were covered in fleas, so I left them at the house. I could only imagine what would have happened if I had been pulled over by the police driving down the road in my underwear. Believe it or not, I was unsuccessful in leaving the fleas at the property. They somehow came home with me and started a new party at my house. So I had to hear my wife bicker and complain for the next few months in addition to everything else. My underwear drive was a complete waste! This mistake does have a happy ending, though, because we were able to put a lien on our former tenant's new house for the damages and lost rent. He refinanced soon afterward and we were paid in full.

An update to this story: Each year, I find a way to bring fleas home. It seems that every summer, I have to show a rental property that has fleas. Now, my wife keeps a big supply of flea treatments to handle the problem!

Lesson Learned:
The lesson of this story is that you should never, ever rent to someone you feel sorry for. Only rent to qualified tenants, not the tenant with the most heartbreaking story. This is a hard lesson to apply because deep down we want to help other people. Try to make your decisions based upon what is the best business move, not on what's the best emotional move. I have learned that I can still help out others outside of my investing. Treat your properties and your tenants as a business! In hindsight, I could have donated furniture or clothes, or even money to the family rather than rent to them.

MISTAKE TWO: Giving your tenant keys before their deposit, up-front payment and/or first month's rent clears the bank.

One of our clients signed a new tenant to a lease agreement and accepted a personal check for the security deposit payment. At this meeting, he gave his happy new tenants the keys. Because this report is about mistakes, you could probably guess that this happy new tenant's check bounced. Three days after he had this new tenant, he had to start eviction procedures. Because the tenant had possession of the home, he was forced to go through the full eviction process. It took our client two months to get this tenant out. The scary part is that he had no security deposit to offset any of his lost money. This one simple mistake cost my client over $3,000. In talking with him, he said that the new tenants seemed like really good people. They were really excited about his house. They also had planned on moving in that day. He didn't want to mess up their moving plans and was trying to help them out. These tenants understood the system game and had no intentions of paying. They just wanted to scam a free place to live for a few months.

Lesson Learned:
The lesson of this story is only accept cash, bank or cashier's checks when signing a lease and turning the keys over. Never give possession to a new tenant until you're positive that their up-front payments, security deposit and first month's rent are good. If you give keys to them, you will have to go through the formal eviction procedures to get them out. NEVER VIOLATE THIS RULE!!

I now tell all of my new tenants on the phone that if they want to get the keys when we sign the lease or the rent-to-own contracts that I need to have them bring cash to the meeting. I tell them before the meeting that if they bring a personal check, I will have to wait until it clears before they can get the keys. Just yesterday, a new tenant brought in a personal check and wanted the keys to start moving that afternoon. Sorry Charlie, no cigar. They left without any keys and are supposed to bring in cash today. We will see!

MISTAKE THREE: Renting to friends or family

I rented one of my units to the sister of one of my best friends. Because of the friendship, I discounted the rent for her. My thought process was that because I discounted the rent, she would take on more responsibility around the property. Unfortunately, she was under a different understanding. I think she felt that because her brother was one of my best friends, I would do more for her than the typical landlord. It really got ugly for a period of time. We both had different expectations as to how things were going to be. The sad part was that I was trying to be nice and save her money by reducing her monthly rent. Because of the differing expectations, my relationship with my best friend was impaired. Many years have gone by now and my friendship has recovered to the way it used to be. However, when I attend his family parties (his kid's birthday parties) and see his sister, my former tenant, it is uncomfortable. His sister and I exchange pleasantries but that is as far as it goes.

Lesson Learned:
The lesson of this story is to never, ever rent to family or friends. Your investing is a business and you should run it as a business. You haven't invested your time and money to help out a friend. You have invested your time and money to earn a nice return on your investment. Anytime you rent to friends or family, you will more than likely lose money and possibly a friendship. Don't knowingly create more headaches for yourself. I follow this rule religiously now. Recently, a new member of my team wanted to rent one of my properties. I really wanted to help him out, but it violated my rule. Today, we have a very good working relationship without any landlord tenant problems.

MISTAKE FOUR: Not training tenants about the rules of the game. (Aka – Setting the tone)

The best way to explain this is to compare it to parenting small children. I have found that when I threaten my daughter without following through on the threat, it has no impact on her behavior. In fact, the behavior that I was trying to stop actually gets worse. She has the incredible ability to see right through me. It's actually the same in a landlord/tenant relationship. If you let a tenant pay late without any repercussions, they automatically begin to pay late from that point forward. If you make a repair at the home that was their responsibility, all future repairs are now your responsibility. When you compromise just one time, you have set yourself up for further compromises. Understand that the first few months of your relationship with your tenant are the most crucial for effective management. If you are friendly and bend the rules, you are shooting yourself in the foot. They will walk all over you. Please have the courage and self-discipline to enforce the rules and set the tone that you are serious and won't take any abuse. If a tenant tells me they will pay the rent by a certain date and I don't have it, I will post an eviction notice on their door that night. If a tenant doesn't pay the rent on the first and hasn't called me to explain what's going on, I call them on the second at 7:00 a.m. to ask where the rent is? Your tenant needs to know at the very beginning of your relationship that you are serious and how you expect things to go each month.

I want my tenants to realize that paying the rent late is not an option. They will have problems with me if it isn't paid as agreed. I would rather have them pay their other bills late, not the rent. From time to time, you will have a tenant call you and ask you to do something that isn't your responsibility.

169

You might want to ignore the call or the message. If you have a hard time telling your tenants "NO," avoid the conversation altogether. When I first started investing, I wanted to be a "Nice" guy. I wanted my tenants to like me. This mind set allowed me to bend the rules and make repairs and updates that weren't my responsibility. Now I try to avoid the conversation altogether by screening their requests. I respond to the valid requests and let the others fall by the wayside.

Lesson Learned:
Train your tenants on how you want them to behave right from the very beginning of your relationship. Sometimes you have to be tough with your tenants in the beginning so that you don't struggle through the entire rental term. If you are lenient to your tenants in the beginning, they will, without question, take advantage of you.

MISTAKE FIVE: Not watching the details

When a tenant calls to notify us of a problem, we have learned to have the tenant get a few estimates for the repair work. We have found that this saves us time and keeps the tenant involved in the process. They send us the quotes and we make the decision on who does what and for how much.

A few years ago, a tenant complained that the furnace wasn't working. One heating contractor noted on his quote that the furnace was older and should be replaced. I simply ignored his suggestion that the furnace should be replaced and had whatever the problem was fixed. In my opinion, just because a furnace is older doesn't mean it should be replaced. A few months later, the tenant's wife called to tell us her husband got burned trying to fix the furnace. Understand, we had the furnace fixed a few months before when they had notified us there was a problem. Also, understand that they never notified us the second time that the furnace wasn't operating properly. The tenant just tried to fix the problem on his own without communicating with us. While in the process of his repair, a flame shot out and burned his arm. We honestly felt terrible that the furnace injured him. A few weeks had passed and our tenant sued us for his injuries. As a landlord, you are only responsible for your tenant's injuries if you are negligent. You are negligent if you are notified of a problem and don't fix it. An example would be if the carpeting on the stairs in your rental property has a hole in it. The tenant tells you about the hole and you don't fix it. If they fall down the steps because of the hole that you knew about, you are responsible because you were negligent in your duties. Our tenant's attorney stated that we were negligent because one of the contractor's quotes from several months earlier read, "furnace is older and should be replaced." This claim was turned over to our homeowner's insurance company and somehow has gone away. I believe it was dropped because there was never any charge against our deductible.

Looking back, I had no way of preventing his injury. I didn't even know that the furnace had stopped working for the second time. However, when we received the earlier quote that stated that the furnace is older and should be replaced, we should have discussed this matter in more depth with the heating contractor. If the furnace truly needed to be replaced, we should have replaced it. If the furnace repair person was just trying to get a new installation job, we should have had him amend his quote to state specifically what was wrong and not allow the quote to say that the furnace should be replaced, or we could have had other contractors inspect the furnace.

Lesson Learned:
The lesson of this story is to always focus on the details of
your investments. When you stop keeping the details in front
of you, you are bound to be taught a similar lesson yourself.

MISTAKE SIX: Trying to save a penny and losing a dollar

Over the years, I have personally made numerous offers on homes for investment. In addition, I have worked with hundreds of clients acquiring investment property. One mistake that we have to continuously try to help our clients avoid is incorrectly walking away from a good deal. During a negotiation on an investment, it is pretty typical to get to a point where you say to yourself, if the seller doesn't take this offer, then the heck with them.

My pride has cost me thousands of dollars over the years. Here is what I mean: Let's say you found a great property that has a market value of $128,000. In your negotiations, your offer is at $118,000 and the seller's counter offer is at $120,000. You offer to increase your price to $119,000, asking the seller to drop down another $1,000. In essence, you're trying to meet the seller in the middle of $118,000 and $120,000. In the past, if the seller said no and stayed at $120,000, I would walk away and go look for another home. I would have made a big mistake because I would have walked away from $8,000 of instant value *for $1,000.*

Lesson Learned:
The lesson from this story is to try to step back during a
negotiation and get a feel for the big picture. Don't focus on
the price you are paying, focus instead on the value you are

receiving. Don't let your pride cost you thousands of dollars. Sometimes you should pay a little more to lock in value at the time of purchase.

MISTAKE SEVEN: The biggest and most costly mistake of All--Not investing in any real estate!

The most costly mistake you can make is not investing in any real estate. As noted in this book, the return on investment from real estate in incredible. It completely blows away the stock market. Not investing in a few properties in the next 12 months can literally cost you a million dollars during your lifetime. I promise that if you do invest in real estate, you will be happy with your choice. I also promise that you will make mistakes. You will mess up. You may even have to drive home in your underwear like I did. I hope not. The mistakes you make are worth it. Would you make 100 mistakes for a million dollars? If you answered yes, then real estate investing is for you. If you answered no, then don't invest!

Lesson Learned:
Stop worrying about making mistakes and get started. Everything will work itself out; it always does.

These are just a few of the things I have learned on my journey as a real estate investor. I really haven't even scratched the surface of mistakes that I have made. Try to learn from your mistakes rather than walking away from them. Make sure that you throw the rock up again, but in a different direction. Use your mistakes as learning opportunities. Remember that if you don't learn the lesson properly the first time, it will be given back to you again. You can dramatically reduce the number of mistakes by getting around and learning from other successful investors. You can learn from their mistakes and avoid making the same ones yourself. In my monthly Income for Life newsletter, I write about common investor challenges and how to overcome them. I share ways to make your investments more profitable and easier to manage. Fill in the form at the end of the book and test-drive this newsletter for yourself!

Now for a strictly Canadian perspective...

Mistakes are part of the game. I now tell our clients to go out and make as many mistakes as possible as quickly as possible.

They're often surprised by this attitude but I now know from experience that mistakes only make you stronger. You learn the best lessons from mistakes. As real estate investors we're fortunate that this type of investing can absorb a lot of mistakes and still turn out with a profit.

Your best teacher will be the mistake you make, so get busy!

I have made almost every mistake mentioned in this chapter plus a few more. Here's another one for you:

MISTAKE EIGHT: Not Following Up With Possible Tenants Quickly

I used to get so excited when a tenant filled out an application for one of my properties that I often went into celebration mode for a few days. I would feel that the job was done and wouldn't follow-up aggressively to sign the leases and collect the upfront option money and first and last month's rent.

On one Rent to Own property I had a very nice young couple fill out the application. Their income looked good and they started talking about how they would furnish the home. She worked as a nurse in the hospital just down the street and he worked as a carpenter and was raving about the workshop in the basement.

I figured this couple was a lock for the home. I took their application on Saturday and went on my merry way until Tuesday when I had some time to check their application. I then called them back on Wednesday, four full days later, and gave them the good news via a voice mail message. They called back the next day and left me a voice mail explaining how excited they were. I then called back and left another voice mail explaining that we needed to meet to collect the upfront deposit money plus first and last month's rent.

A full week had gone by at this point and I was getting calls from other possible tenants who had seen the house. I explained that the house was taken and they would have to look for some else. This was another mistake!

After a few more days of voice mail tag the young couple finally dropped off the face of the earth all together. I had wasted a week and a half chasing them.

At this point I had no money from them, I had turned away all my other leads and I had lost all momentum. It was discouraging. Very discouraging.

Remember, I had paid money for some classified ads to generate these leads. I had invested my time by going to the property and gathering applications. Time away from my family. I had wasted time and money. Not good.

Since most of the people who called on my original ad had now ended up renting out something else, I had to spend money on new advertising.

I ended up placing a new ad and getting back out to the property. This time when a possible tenant filled out the application I called them back the very next day. I also prepared them by explaining I would check their application that night and then call them the next day before lunch.

When I called them with the good news that they had been accepted I immediately setup a time later that day or the very next day to meet me to hand off a deposit cheque for the property. Even if they did not have the entire deposit available that quickly I would ask for partial payment.

I've found that when money has exchanged hands all of a sudden the tenants become very engaged in the process and rarely disappear.

In the end I managed to collect even more money upfront from the new tenant I had found. He offered $7,500 instead of the $5,000 the disappearing couple had offered me. He also gave me first and last month's rent before he moved in.

This all still occurred before my first mortgage payment. I had collected over $10,000 from my tenant before handing over the keys to the house. It was a good feeling.

Lesson Learned:

Never dilly dally. When someone is interested in your house take action! We all get busy and sometimes you can get caught up in non-productive activities. When investing in Rent to Own properties, a tenant/buyer can represent tens of thousands of dollars in profit to you. Move quickly and sign them up. We have all mentioned this throughout the book, it is obviously a very key point.

I now have taken it a step further and ask for a deposit on the home from the tenant right on the spot. Even if they have no cheques on them I'll ask them how much cash they have in their pockets. It's amazing how smoothly things go when a tenant hands over some money to you. They are now invested into the property, literally and emotionally.

Some of my clients have taken this to the next level and gone to the bank with the tenant and collect $5000 in cash from them right away. It's amazing what you can get when you ask for it!

As an aside, sometimes I'm asked how we can possibly collect $5,000 upfront from a tenant. All the properties we deal with are nice homes in nice areas. Sometimes the house will be the nicest one on the street. Tenants are usually in shock that they can rent such a good home. Because our product is so good it's not difficult to get thousands in upfront option money.

Someone once told me that you don't have to get things right you just have to get them going. They were right.

So go ahead and make your mistakes. If you're not making any mistakes you're likely not growing financially or personally.

"If you don't make mistakes, you're not working on hard enough problems. And that's a big mistake."
- Frank Wilcezek, 2004 Nobel Prize Winner in Physics

14

Will You or Won't You?
That Is the Million Dollar Question

If you have read this far, you probably understand that real estate can dramatically change your life. The sad truth is that many of you will not ever invest in real estate. I was listening to a tape program by Dan Kennedy called "Renegade Millionaire." Dan is a consultant who helps business owners grow their businesses. Dan has helped hundreds of his clients become millionaires some even multi-millionaires. In this Renegade Millionaire Program, Dan was asked what was the common denominator amongst his Renegade Millionaire clients. One of the common denominators he found in all of his millionaire clients was that they owned real estate as an investment. Dan is not a real estate investing guru, although he is a real estate investor. He is a business consultant. He helps business owners increase their income and wealth. The "Renegade Millionaire Program was not about real estate investing. However, it was specifically stated that each successful client had also invested in real estate.

Tony Robbins has been known for saying that "Success Leaves Clues." I guess the opposite would also be true: "Poverty Leaves Clues." How many poor people do you know that own real estate investments? I personally don't know of any poor people who arc rcal cstate investors. If the Renegade Millionaires own real estate and the poor people don't, which do you think is a better course of action? It is simple, really. Find out what wealthy people do and then do the same thing.

Why most people don't start investing…

From my years of helping real estate investors, I have found that the majority of people want to invest in real estate but are fearful. I would venture to say that most people never get what they want in life because fear stops them. In essence, they are afraid of making a mistake, looking foolish, getting taken advantage of, or the big one—losing money.

Authors Jack Canfield and Mark Victor Hansen in their book *How to Live Your Dreams* say, "Fear is self-created by imagining catastrophic consequences that have yet to happen. It is all in your mind. If the clock strikes midnight and your teenage son or daughter is not yet home, you may begin to imagine them wrapped around a tree, drunk at a party, or being taken advantage of sexually. You can scare yourself by imagining all of these images……. Stop the catastrophic thoughts and images, and the fear goes away. You are going to have to stop imagining failure and take some risks."

I can appreciate that you might be fearful of investing in real estate. I was petrified for my first investment property. I bought my first rental property when I was 23. There was not a single person in my family who had ever owned real estate as an investment. Neither my grandparents, aunts and uncles, nor my parents had owned any investment real estate. None of my friends had invested in real estate. I didn't have anyone to act as a model. All I had to go from was the books that I had read. I didn't even have the 10% down payment needed to buy my first property. I had to borrow it from my mother. She was, and still remains, very supportive of my goals and dreams. However, I was so fearful that I wouldn't be able to repay her down payment loan.

When I made the offer to buy my first property, I was so nervous I was shaking. The offer was accepted quickly, making me feel that I overpaid. During the closing process, I wanted to back out several times but didn't. When the title finally transferred into my name, I had trouble sleeping at night. For some reason, I kept on thinking of all the things that could go wrong. In hindsight, I should have stayed focused on all of the income streams I was creating. Instead, I was worried about….

- Would the tenants like me as their landlord?
- Would the tenants take care of the property?
- What would happen to me if they didn't pay the rent?
- What happens if they decide to move out?
- How will I find good tenants?
- What happens if I can't cover the mortgage payment and my monthly payment to my mother?
- What happens if there is a fire or storm that damages my home?
- What happens if I get sued?

In reality, I was "What If-ing myself to death…." How about changing my what ifs to something like this….

- What if the value of my home doubles in five years? What would I do with the profit?
- What if the tenants want to make improvements to my home?
- What if I take the monthly cash flow and save it in a savings account for down payments on other properties?
- What if I raise the rents; how much more money can I make?

- What if I pay extra each month on the mortgage; how quickly can I get this property paid off?
- What if I install coin operated laundry machines; how much more could I make?
- Could I rent out the garage for additional rental income?

I hope that you can see that you must control your thinking. Most people have been programmed throughout their lives to look for the worst possible thing that could happen. The outcome of the investment was going to be dependent upon the way I was thinking. Had I stayed in the fearful mindset, every little thing would have caused me alarm. Thankfully, I was able to switch my mindset to look for opportunity instead of looking for problems.

How to get out of the fearful mindset!

In some very helpful reflective thinking, I now realize what helped my move away from fear. I remember asking myself, "What is the absolute worst thing that can happen to me from buying this investment property?" My answer was that the property burned down in a fire. Well, that wouldn't be too bad because I had homeowner's insurance on the property. The insurance policy would kick in and rebuild the home. I was also worried about a tenant vandalizing the home. It dawned on me that the homeowner's insurance policy also covered vandalism.

My next concern was, "The tenants could move out and I wouldn't have any income to cover the monthly mortgage payments." This investment had two units, an upstairs and a down stairs unit. More than likely, both units wouldn't be vacant at the same time. I would probably have at least $500 a month coming in from one of the units. The total payment, including the monthly payment to my mother, was around $850. I thought that I might have to ask my mother for a month's grace period to get the other unit rented. When that unit was rented, I would make up the missed payment plus the new payment. I realized that I would get a security deposit plus first month's rent from my new tenant. This would provide me with about $1,000 of income. This would make up any missed payments to my mother.

Another fear of owning real estate was being sued. I asked myself, if I were sued and lost, how would I pay for the loss? In my homeowner's insurance policy for the property, there was rider for liability. I think the normal policy coverage provided $100,000 of liability protection. I decided to have this limit raised to $300,000. I then learned about umbrella insurance policies and the higher protection they provide. I paid for a $2 million umbrella insurance policy. It only cost me about $250 a year. With these two moves, I protected myself against a $2 million claim. Understand that if I am negligent in some way, these policies will not provide any help. However, I wasn't worried about being negligent. I knew that I would be a responsible landlord. I wasn't afraid of my actions. I could control my actions, just not someone else's.

I now use other strategies to protect my assets. These strategies are detailed in my monthly real estate investing newsletter. For me, my fears about investing in real estate were all smoke and mirrors. There was a solution to each fear that I had. My job and your job as a real estate investor is to use your fears to reduce your risk. I recommend that you take each fear you have and figure out a way to do something that will eliminate the possible problem. In other words, use your fear productively. Protect yourself; don't just ignore your fear.

The rest of the story on my first investment property purchase….

My first investment property that was keeping me up at night was a brick two-family home in Euclid. I think that I paid $83,000 for it. Both tenants had been in the home for several years and were paying below market rents. I had read in one of the investing books that the best time to raise your tenant's rents is right when you buy the property. The book told me that the tenants always expected a rent increase when the property sells. The book didn't tell me not to raise the rent too much all at once. I raised each tenant's rent over $50 each month. Can you guess what happened?

You got it--both tenants decided to move out of the home. The fearful me would have panicked! Instead, I decided to take the time to renovate each unit when it was vacant. My best friend and I painted every wall, replaced the carpeting, and installed new tile floors. After each unit was renovated, I was able to rent them at much higher monthly rents. When it was all said and done, the property's value was dramatically increased because of the improvements and higher monthly rents. The property was more profitable every month and I had new tenants in the property that I selected, rather than two tenants inherited from the previous owner.

My biggest fear turned into one of the best opportunities.

When I was in the process of buying this investment property, one of my friends got very excited about investing in real estate. I had told him about a few of the books I was reading. He started to read them, too. He was also fearful of getting started and losing money. Unfortunately, he never overcame his fears. He never got started investing. Even to this day, he doesn't own any real estate investments. Once in a while, I wonder how his life would be today had he challenged himself to face his fear. I think he may have to work hard his whole life to be able to afford to retire. I really truly wish he had started investing. He could have let his properties work hard so that he wouldn't have to.

Now when I become fearful about an investing decision, I ask myself, "What is the worst thing that can happen to me?" If the answer is something that I can live with, I move forward with the investment. If the answer is something that I can't live with, I don't move forward with the investment. It is a simple tool I use to decide what to do and what not to do.

If I decide to move forward with the investment, I then list all of my fears and concerns and I brainstorm ways to reduce and minimize each fear or concern. I ask myself, how can I reduce or eliminate this fear or concern? I then list every single idea that pops in my mind. Some of them are bad ideas, but some of them are good ideas. I then pick the best ideas and I go to work to implement them into my approach. In many cases, the answers are right in front of me. In others, you have to search and keep focused. They come eventually. My guess is that this same process could also be helpful for you.

The challenge is to follow Nike's philosophy and "Just Do It." Everything will eventually work itself out. It always does. I hope that you conquer your fears and get started. If you do, we would love to hear from you!

Now for a strictly Canadian perspective...

You will never run from your fear but we described a very advanced strategy for dealing with it. I recommend three things when you are thinking about Real Estate investing:

#1 Decide

Decide. Pretty simple. You must decide that you want to invest and the decision must be your own. I often see people start doing something without making a 100% commitment to it.

Then, at the first sign of any issue, no matter how small, they run for the hills. When I see people invest who have clearly made a firm decision with themselves they do not let anything stand in their way. Those are the people who reap the rewards.

One client I was working with could not bring himself to buy an investment property after months of looking because of some arcane mathematical formula that he was using. He was taking the average property tax rates in the area and measuring that against the recent purchases and against the home he was thinking of buying.

When the calculation returned a result that was off by a decimal point, he walked away from the house and walked away from investing all together!!

I had another client who bought the identical home in the same area and collected $7,000 upfront and has positive cash flow on the property.

The first client had not decided he was going to invest. He had all the knowledge, he had a team of experienced people around him and somehow managed to talk himself out of it.

The second client made a decision. He decided he was going to be an investor. He collected the education he needed, surrounded himself by the right team of people and then took action. Nothing was going to stop him. Nothing.

Make your decision. Do you want to be in the game or do you want to watch?

#2 Write Down The Worst Thing That Could Happen

If you are having trouble making your decision you should really do as suggested earlier. Write out all the things that you are scared of happening.

Then next to each write out what you could do to protect yourself from it.

Fire? Buy insurance.

Can't find tenants? Find an investor to learn from.

Scared you may have to evict? Type in 'landlord tenant board' in Google and read about it. It's all well laid out for you.

Not sure what contracts to use for a rent to own? Find a lawyer or investor who focuses on real estate. They exist, right here in Ontario and all over Canada.

Can't find a good investor mortgage? Find a mortgage broker who deals with investors. Many brokers know of special mortgages specifically designed for investors.

Worried about damage to your property? Use Rent to Own strategies to collect thousands of dollars up front, this way you have money in the bank to protect you from any losses. Then visit the Landlord Tenant Board. You can evict someone for damaging your property. Talk to your insurance company for proper coverage.

What else is on your mind? Write it down and brainstorm a few ideas.

If you can live with the worst then you have taken a big step towards moving forward. You'll feel confident with your decision.

#3 Attention

Look, you only have as much attention as you can give. If you focus all of it on worrying or on endless learning you will get nowhere. Read the previous two sentences again.

You need to put your attention towards taking action.

Go get some good information on real estate investing. Then surround yourself with a good team.

I have learned that the best information is not nearly as valuable as a team of experienced people around me. A good mentor, an excellent broker, an experienced lawyer and a savvy accountant are invaluable.

Then take action. That's it. It really is. Stop trying to make things more difficult than they are.

I see too many people putting their attention on going to just one more seminar, or just reading one more book, or speaking to one more family member, or jumping up and down or running in circles.

Stop it. Put your attention on taking action. Experience is the best teacher. You know it's true.

So make your decision and then put your attention on taking action.

You only have so much attention every day. If you put it towards activities that don't move you forward you are wasting time.

Go do something productive, go now!

190

15

How You Can Create a Million Dollars for Your Retirement or Your Child's Financial Freedom

Doesn't it seem that every once in a while you hear some fantastic idea that has the ability to drastically change your life. Well, I want to share one of the ideas that I have been working on that has changed my life and hopefully my family's as well. *This idea is focused on providing for your children; however, if you don't have any children, you can use the same concept to fund your own IRA.* Most parents want to provide a better life for their children than they have had. Today it seems that most financial planners recommend that you should be focused on saving for your retirement, rather than investing to help your child with college, or for your child's retirement, for that matter. The financial advisors tell you to make sure your savings are on track before saving for someone else.

One of my goals when I became a father was to try to make sure that my daughter was financially independent. As I learned and studied various ideas, I started to try different techniques. I finally formulated an idea that just blew me away. The best part about this idea is that you can help your children and yourself at the same time. *With this one idea, you could improve your retirement and ensure that your child becomes financially independent.*

The underlying concept of this idea is to get money invested into an IRA today for your retirement or your child's financial future. Using the compounding benefits over time, your child would become a millionaire without much effort. We like to teach our clients to set up automatic systems to build wealth. When I say automatic, I mean that it doesn't take much effort to maintain the system once it's in place. Or another way to look at it is to work once and get paid over and over again from your efforts.

Compare the homebuilder to the writer. The homebuilder has to build a house to get paid. The only way the homebuilder gets paid again is by building another house. This process must continue for the homebuilder to earn money. The writer, on the other hand, writes one book and gets paid again and again for his or her efforts as the book sells over time.

Many people try to save the hard way. They go to work and when they get their paycheck they try to put some money aside for savings or investments. The only way they get more money into their savings is to go to work again to earn another paycheck and save a portion of this new paycheck. However, in today's economy it is very hard to build your savings this way. Just when you get some money put aside, something happens and you need to dip into your savings for whatever reason. The end result is that you have to start back from scratch saving money from your paycheck.

Instead focus on setting up a system that saves for you. This concept is extremely important. When you have a system save for you, you don't have to struggle by setting aside money from your paycheck every month. You still can and probably should set aside money from your paycheck, but if you don't save this month from your paycheck, your system is still saving for your goals automatically.

Try using this approach to set up an automatic savings program for any financial goal you may have. Buy one single-family rental property and earn money from positive cash flow and appreciation throughout the upcoming years. Consider investing this monthly cash flow and appreciation toward your financial goal or your child's retirement. Because your child is so far away from retiring, this money will compound substantially over time without much effort on your part.

To make this idea even better, when you buy your single-family rental home, hand a flyer to prospective tenants when you show the home. In this flyer, drop in a picture of your child. Put a cute little slogan underneath like *"Please rent this home from my dad/mom."* I know you're thinking, this sounds real tacky. Here is why you should consider having your child model in your flyers: <u>You can pay them for the services rendered</u>. What this means to you is that you can pay your child for their modeling services. This payment to your child is a tax deduction for you as an advertising expense in your rental business. With this income, your child has earned income and can open a Roth IRA. If you don't know, a Roth IRA is tax free for life! So you have now invested in your child's retirement and received a tax deduction for your efforts. This is like getting your cake and eating it too. Your child will now have taxable income from the money earned. However, can you think of a way to offset your child's income? How about an IRA? Your child can contribute his income into their own IRA. Depending on the type of IRA selected, your child's IRA contribution may offset the taxable income that they received for their modeling services. The only two requirements someone needs to have an IRA are:

1. Have Earned Income
2. Have a Social Security Number

Many young children don't have earned income, so they aren't eligible for an IRA account. With this strategy, your child now has earned income and can contribute to an IRA. Your baby's picture could be included in your rental property marketing efforts. If you could start using this strategy very early in your child's life, the results would be astronomical.

So let's take a step back for a second and analyze what we have done. What you have done is receive a tax deduction for investing money in your child's IRA. I don't know about you, but this really makes a lot of sense to me.

I have now laid down a challenge for myself. My challenge is to ensure that my daughter would become a millionaire without having to give money to her out of my own pocket. This is what I started with: I bought one single-family rental property and I included her picture in the flyer and advertising of this home. For her modeling services, I will pay her $150 a month. She will invest that money into her own IRA. We started this arrangement when she turned one. She is now three and has about $2,600 in her IRA. Assuming that I continue to use her modeling services and pay her $150 a month for the next five years, she will have accumulated $14,400 in her IRA. Now remember, she will be eight years old at this time. For discussion purposes, let's assume no other contributions will be made after age eight into her IRA. If this $14,400 is invested at 12% per year, when she is 50 years old, her IRA will be worth $1,680,813. What are my odds of meeting my challenge of guaranteeing that she becomes financially independent? For me, the best part is that I get to keep the home for additional income in my retirement and she gets to become a millionaire. Not a bad deal, is it? After she turns eight, I can use the $150 a month for my own savings program.

Do you see how the savings program was automatic? Not one penny of the $150 monthly modeling fee came out of my pocket. It was paid from the rental income that my property earned. Compare this to saving $150 each month from a regular paycheck.

We had a meeting in our office recently and I posed the following question to my team. I asked them, is it easier to make money or create money? Many people are so busy making money at their jobs that they don't learn ways to create money. I have obviously used some assumptions in my planning, such as the 12% return from age eight to age 50. What happens if I fall short? What happens if her IRA only earns 10% per year? If I fall short, she still wins. What if I am only able to create $850,000 of money? Who loses? Remember that you don't have to invest a penny of your own money into this account. You created this money through one of your investments. If you fall short, children will have $850,000 at retirement without having to save a penny of their own money. If they did the same thing for their kids, you would be leaving a legacy to your family.

The big question to consider is "Can you set up a system to create money that would help your child become financially independent?" Well, here is my big challenge to you: "Can you make your child a millionaire?" What would your life be like today if your parents had followed a similar approach when you were a child?

I have been asking myself another question lately. Is it more important to save for your child's college education or for their retirement/financial independence? I don't think I have ever heard anyone recommend that you should save for your child's retirement. My thought is that my child's financial independence is more important than having college paid for in advance. The way I see it, my child can get student loans to pay for college and I can take care of the financial independence part. To me, it doesn't really matter what my child does for a career, or what school she should go to, as long as she is happy. If she knows she will be financially independent, she can make drastically different decisions throughout her life. She won't feel forced to take a job she won't enjoy because of financial need. She will have the ability to follow her dreams rather than a paycheck. My focus has shifted from saving for her college to saving for her financial independence.

If this sounds like a good idea to you, I recommend that you get started right now. Don't wait, because starting a year from now can cost thousands to your child at age 50. <u>As always, discuss these strategies with your tax and legal counsel to be sure they are appropriate for your situation.</u>

Now for a strictly Canadian perspective...

Now that you have learned to think outside the box with the Rent to Own investment philosophy, what better time to introduce another unique idea.

Many professional financial advisors and accountants will preach the wonders of compound interest and the power it has to make your investment portfolio grow. And the single most powerful factor with compound interest is time.

Let's pretend that the average age someone starts to contribute to their RRSP is 25 and you decide to start implementing this great idea at age 5. You have just added 20 years of time to your child's investments and tens of thousands of dollars in income.

If only $150 is invested every month at 10% in those twenty years the investment will be worth just under $115 000. They will be that much further ahead plus when the interest compounds on that amount it will continue to grow at a much faster pace than starting out at age 25. What are you waiting for?

Investing in a Rent to Own home now has two huge purposes and impacts on your life. It will not only build your net worth and income it can also build your child's net worth.

I would recommend speaking with an accountant or lawyer to confirm that everything you put in place is ideal for your specific situation. My research has shown me that a child of any age can obtain a Social Insurance Number and once income is made there can be a contribution into the RRSP plan for you child. But again it is always best to discuss with an expert.

In Canada we also have the RESP that is specifically geared towards saving for your child's schooling. This can also be a beneficial way to contribute towards this plan. I would examine the benefits of both.

Personally I think building an asset base for my child is the most important legacy I can leave. It can be a life changer because it can give them the flexibility to free themselves from the 'rat race' at an earlier age. This to me, is invaluable.

But here is an even better idea. We sometimes see our clients move tentatively towards their first investment property (but they do follow the most important rule and 'take action'). After their first one they take their new found level of confidence and buy at least one more property.

If you have two properties why not use one property as a source of income for your child's education and the second as a vehicle for building long term wealth?

With all the new Canadian investment property mortgage programs available this is not hard to make happen.

Amazingly, it all comes back to taking action. We can talk about it until your child is ready for college or university and then wonder 'what if' or you can decide to do something about it now.

You decide.

16

The Ultimate Investing Secret

As a real estate investor, you need to know what makes a property an *asset* or a *liability*. For many years, I thought the property's numbers determined if it was an asset or liability. What I mean is that if the property's rental income was higher than the expenses, I assumed it was an *asset*. If the property's expenses were higher than its income, I assumed it was a *liability*. This thought process of mine continued for many years until I realized the secret of what makes an investment an asset or a liability. Here is the big secret I finally learned ...

A property is just a property. You can change the property's market value by seeing opportunity where others don't.

You, as the investor, make all the difference in the world. Truly successful investors are able to make their properties more valuable. They are able to, in essence, create money out of the thin blue air. Consider how Donald Trump can improve the value of a property just by putting his name on it. This was one of those BIG lessons in life for me. You are probably asking, *"How do successful investors create money?"*

THEY THINK DIFFERENTLY
THAN UNSUCCESSFUL INVESTORS

I find that I am able to grasp concepts much better if they are tied into a real life story. So I will share a real life story to help you understand the big secret that you can actually increase the value of your property.

A partner and I bought a seven-unit building. The seller had owned this building for about 15 years. As we researched the building, we learned that the rents were low and there was space in this building to rent out as another separate unit. When we crunched the numbers, the building was only worth about $230,000 based on its rents and expenses at that time. However, we felt that we could increase this building's value dramatically by increasing the rental income. An investment property's value is really based upon its income and expenses. If you can increase the income, the market value increases 10-fold. We paid $300,000 for the building. We owned this building for about four years and resold it for $425,000. The reason it took us four years was because five of the units were commercial with longer-term leases. We had to wait until each of these leases ended to increase the rent for that unit.

Here is how we did it:

We increased the rents from the seven units from $3,700 per month to $4,200. We split one of the units into two separate rental units, which increased the rental income by another $425 per month. So the monthly rental income increase was $925, which totaled $11,000 annually. This annual increase in rental income increased this property's value by about $111,000. We also increased the value further by selling it with owner financing. We offered a low down payment and an attractive interest rate, which increased the number of buyers that would be interested. We had several offers on this property when we sold it.

Now, can you start to see how we were able to see value where the previous owner couldn't? Let me also tell you that this wasn't all that easy. We lost a few tenants in the process, which meant showing, advertising and lost rents. We rented to some people that we shouldn't have. It was extremely hard work, but in the end it really paid off.

Once I learned the lesson that the investor can increase value, I wanted to see if I could create more value on single-family homes. This is how I got started using Rent-to-Own programs. Rent-to-Own programs increase the demand. Higher demand means more monthly rent. More monthly rent means increased market value.

IT REALLY BOILS DOWN TO THIS:

TO MAKE YOUR INVESTMENT MORE VALUABLE, YOU MUST:

INCREASE THE DEMAND FOR YOUR PROPERTY

The more ways you're able to increase the demand for your property, the more profitable your investing will be. Here are a few ways to consider:

1. A friend and client of mine bought a single-family home on two separate lots. After he closed on his purchase, he offered to sell the extra buildable lot. He sold this lot for $15,000 and kept the home to rent out on a Rent-To-Own program. He created demand by offering a separate buildable lot that wasn't previously available. He also created demand on the home by offering a Rent-To-Own program.

2. We live near Lake Erie. I have heard that there is an investor who buys older homes that are lakefront, or have a lake view. This investor then remodels the home and puts in as many windows facing the lake as possible. By increasing the lake views from the home, he increases the number of buyers that would want to buy the home. More demand, more value.

3. One client of mine bought a home situated on a lot that was populated with trees. We just happened to find out that a few of these trees were Black Walnut. I had no clue, but this wood is very valuable. He was offered over $10,000 for just the Black Walnut trees. He created demand by seeing value that nobody else was able to see.

4. Offering seller financing on a home. If a buyer doesn't have to go to the bank to get a loan to buy your home, the home becomes available to more buyers. Some buyers can't get bank financing. When you offer seller financing, you increase demand substantially on your property.

Here is a story of what I mean:

Recently, I encountered a seller who lives out of state trying to sell a property locally. The property is paid for in full, and there is no mortgage on the property. The seller has been waiting for a buyer who can pay cash or obtain bank financing. She keeps lowering her price to increase demand. If she would offer to finance the sale, she could get substantially more in price, plus earn additional money on the interest charged to the buyer. Since she is unwilling to do this, could you buy her home from her and then mark up the price by 40% to 50% and sell with owner financing? You would take something with no demand and make high demand for it. You would be literally creating money by simply increasing demand.

In a nutshell…..

To be successful as a real estate investor, you must challenge yourself to see opportunities that other people don't see. The next time you go look at a property, challenge yourself to figure out at least five ways to increase the demand on the home. By increasing demand, you literally create money. You should even do this mental exercise on properties you don't plan to acquire because it strengthens your vision. When you can see value when others don't, you have become a successful investor.

Now for a strictly Canadian perspective…

This lesson applies to many aspects of life. There are always a number of ways that you can look at things. Instead of choosing the most common or the 'standard' view of a situation, invest a bit of time into your thoughts. Use this time to ask yourself these questions: What else can be done? What angle am I missing?

This way of thinking has often been the cause of huge discoveries. If everyone saw the same thing we may still believe the world is flat. Alright that example may be a bit extreme but did it get my point across?

Successful people look at what can be done differently, that is how you should look at your investments too. It can open up many possibilities.

Often I will see a property that has been totally renovated sit on the market for weeks. The house is a 'flip'. That means that someone bought low and fixed it up to sell it for profit.

The problem is until it sells there is typically a lot of money tied up in the property. And because it sits they end up taking a lower offer than they thought. Sometimes people just don't want to pay market value because they don't like that other people are making money at their expense.

If these 'flippers' knew how to look at things differently they could make quick and drastic changes to their cash flow crunch.

I have filled houses with tenant/buyers here in Ontario in only a couple of weeks. This means I received money upfront, positive cash flow, paid no commissions, and locked in future profit. What if these people chose that route? They would have the same benefits.

These experiences made me start thinking (differently, of course). Why is it that only one investor can make money off a property? Once the property is fixed up it is ideal for a Rent to Own tenant/buyer. And if the property sits on the market the sellers may be motivated. This makes it an even better investment. I can get the home below market value and it will be like new inside. I can make money off of their investment!

This was a breakthrough to me because the standard way of thinking was 'they did a lot of work I wonder how much money was made from their investment?' I should have been thinking, 'Nice house! How can I make money from this opportunity?'

Those are two drastically different statements. One will help you continually move forward and the other will allow you to watch others do things around you.

Remember to constantly be trying to look at things differently and soon it will just become natural. You will stop seeing things from only one angle and instead you will explore them from many.

This skill alone can change many aspects of your life. Now that you know it you have two options, turn the page and don't do anything about it or choose to act!

Only taking action will make a difference for you.

206

17

Do You Want to
Guarantee YOUR Success?

This chapter is to teach you how to know before you buy an investment property if you will make money or not. I am attempting to give you a magical crystal ball in this last chapter. Earlier in the book, I explained that the "Right Property Attracts the Right Tenant." I suggested that you should look for properties that the best tenants would want. This is slightly different than the typical approach investors take. They go try to find a deal (any deal) and then hope they can sell or rent the property for a profit. In fact, many "Real Estate Investing Gurus" who sell these high-priced real estate investing programs teach investors to put up signs that read "I BUY HOUSES" or to mail letters to sellers with hopes of getting a good deal.

I speak from experience on these strategies because I have a box of "We BUY Houses" signs in my office. I have mailed postcards to sellers in hopes of them calling me to come take their home off of their hands. I got a lot of calls from people who had homes that would be a big challenge to rent. In fact, I would venture to guess that you would need to be a full-time investor to make this approach work. You would have to work very hard to get these homes rented or sold because the majority of them don't match what the tenant/buyer market wants.

If you have 50 to 60 hours a week to spend working with this type of property, this approach is fine and dandy, but understand that you are taking on undue risk with these properties because you have no idea if you can resell the home for a profit. In a sense, you are seller-focused instead of buyer-focused. A really good real estate investor focuses on what his customer wants. Good investors invest in the types of properties that most tenant/buyers would want.

To help our investor clients guarantee their profits before they buy an investment property, we have begun to build tenant/buyer lists in our office. In fact, we will be having prospective tenant buyers go through a qualification process including completing an application and explaining to us the type of home they would like to buy using a Rent-to-Own program. If the prospective tenant's application is accepted, we will then find a property for sale that meets the accepted applicant's criteria. We will provide our investor client with the accepted tenant/buyer application and the homes for sale that match the approved tenant's wish list. The goal is to get a non-refundable deposit from the prospective tenant before they even buy the home.

The goal of this process is to have your home sold to a tenant/buyer on a Rent-to-Own program before you buy the property or invest any money. Can you see how this is a reversal of the typical investing process? We want to find a qualified tenant/buyer first and then find a home for that qualified tenant/buyer. Most investors buy the home first and then try to find a qualified tenant/buyer afterward. Both ways work; however, one provides for more safety and ultimately more profits.

The reason the "reverse process" provides more profits is because you can start to receive rental income the day you close on your investment property. You can have your contracts with your tenant/buyers signed in advance and then on your day of closing meet with them to collect the first month's rent and give them the keys. No advertising, no showing, no calls, no hassles.

Your property would be rented just as you got the keys yourself. Most investors have to wait several weeks before they receive any income from their property. By collecting the rent the same day of closing, you could put a few thousand dollars extra in your pocket!

I have heard many people say, "If I had a crystal ball 15 years ago, I would have bought Microsoft stock and been a billionaire today!" Would you buy a stock today for $15 if you knew in advance that you had a buyer for the stock at $20? Of course you would because you would have a locked-in profit of $5 on each share.

The "reverse approach" to real estate investing is your crystal ball. Your profit is locked in before you even buy the home. You know your profits in advance. Would you invest in this home at 123 XYZ Street at $120,000 if I had a qualified rent-to-own buyer that would buy the home at 123 XYZ Street for $140,000? It quite frankly is a no brainer. You would have to be an idiot not to make money in real estate with this approach.

I have tried to save the best for last in this book. Many people would invest in real estate if they knew they couldn't lose. I have just shown you how to not lose in real estate. In just a few paragraphs I have given you a crystal ball. The question now is will you use it?

Will you create Income for Life by investing in real estate? Or will you put the book down and continue doing the same things you have been doing? My guess is that if you have read this far in the book, you are a take-action person. I hope that you take action and start adding multiple income streams into your life.

To help you get started, we have two special resources at the at the end of this book. Good luck, and I wish you years of income!

Now for a strictly Canadian perspective...

The strategy here is excellent and we now have our members here in Ontario doing exactly this. It really does change the game and tilt the scales in your favour.

You almost guarantee your success with a strategy like this and some of our members have maximized their profits to truly amazing levels by doing it.

To help you get started, we have two special resources at the end of this book.

Good luck and I wish you years of income!

Special Gift #1 from the Authors
Copy this Page and Fax this Form to: 416-981-3467
www.YourRockStarLife.com/OneDollar.html
$1 Rock Star Inner Circle Membership
Test Drive 1 Month of Tom & Nick Karadza's
Rock Star Inner Circle Membership
Receive a steady stream of investing advice

 Yes, I want to lock up a trial membership in your Rock Star Inner Circle, which includes:

1. ROCK STAR INNER CIRCLE WEEKLY REPORTS
2. ROCK STAR INNER CIRCLE BONUS REPORTS
3. BONUS AUDIO INTERVIEWS WITH INVESTMENT PROFESSIONALS
4. ACCESS TO PHONE IN CONSULTATIONS
5. CURRENT DAY AGREEMENTS TOM & NICK USE FOR THEIR REAL ESTATE INVESTMENTS

[You have no obligation to continue at the lowest Member price of $27.00 per month. In fact, should you continue with your membership, you can cancel at any time by calling The Inner Circle office at 905-338-6964 or faxing a cancellation note to 416-981-3467] Remember, your credit card will NOT be charged the low monthly $27.00 until the 1st of the 2nd month, which means you have until the end of the third month to read, test, and **profit from all of the powerful techniques and strategies you get from being a Rock Star Inner Circle Member.** And of course, it's impossible for you to lose, because if you don't absolutely LOVE everything you get, you can simply cancel your membership before the end of the month and we will even refund the $1 you paid.

Name _____ Business Name _____

Address _____ City _____

Province ____ Postal Code _____ E-mail _____

Phone _____ Fax _____

Credit Card: ___American Express ___Visa ___MasterCard

Credit Card No. _____ Expiration Date _____

Signature _____ Date _____

Providing this information constitutes your permission for Karadza Publishing Inc.
to contact you regarding information via mail, e-mail, fax, and phone.

Special Free Gift #2 from the Authors

FREE Real Estate Investing Articles, Tips, Opinions...

 Yes, I want to learn as much as possible about Real Estate investing! $197 Value.

VISIT:

www.TheRealEstateRenegades.com/book

To sign up for a courtesy subscription to the author's "Renegade Real Estate Investing Newsletter". Just some of the topics include:

- **How to find** properties right here in Canada that make you money

- What you should know about **"buying into demand"** versus "speculating" or "flipping"

- The **most common mistakes** all beginner investors make!

- Real Estate investment tips about investment mortgages and the **latest developments** in the Canadian mortgage markets.

- How to build a **network of professionals** that will watch your back

- How to easily **increase demand** for any of your investments

- Why "systems" are more important than **any other** tips and why they are almost always overlooked

Special Free Gift #3 from the Authors
Copy This Page and Fax this Form to: 416-981-3467
FREE Gift
$124.80 Value Information Package

Special Reports

1. **How to Build Wealth Using Your RRSP to Invest in Real Estate.**
Throughout this book various investing approaches have been discussed. A key concept is having your houses buy more houses. This audio report that Tom put together will explain how you can invest in Real Estate using funds in your RRSP. (Sold separately for $99.95)

2. **How to Become Financial Independent in 7 Months.** In this audio recording, Rob interviews a client who generated enough monthly income from his investments in 7 months that he was able to retire from his $100,000 a year corporate job. Many beginning investors feel that it will take several years for them to have enough money to quit their jobs. This simply isn't true. In this interview, you will hear how this investor became free so quickly. (Sold separately for $19.95)

3. **How to Make Your Phone Ring Off the Hook.** This special report reveals detailed tips and strategies for effectively marketing your home to your tenants. The specific examples and shortcuts will wipe out your learning curve saving you countless hours and money. (Sold Separately for $29.95).

4. **How to Get Rich Audio Presentation.** A presentation Rob gave to a group of investors detailing specific steps to build your wealth investing in real estate. In this presentation, Rob discusses a very common costly mistake that most investors make and how you can avoid it yourself. (Sold Separately for $24.95)

To Obtain this Free Information Package: There is no need to damage your book by tearing out this Coupon – a photocopy is satisfactory. Complete ALL the information required, then either fax this form to (416) 981-3467 or mail to Karadza Publishing Inc, Suite #1467, 1011 Upper Middle Road East, Oakville, ON, L6H 5Z9.

Name _____ Business Name_____

Address _____ City_____

Province____ Postal Code_____ E-mail_____

Phone _____ Fax_____

Providing this information constitutes your permission for Karadza Publishing Inc. to contact you regarding information via mail, e-mail, fax, and phone.

The authors of this book can be contacted regarding other information, products, or services at the following addresses:

Tom Karadza
Nick Karadza
1011 Upper Middle Road East
Suite 1467
Oakville, Ontario, L6H 5Z9
Phone: 905-338-6964 Fax: 416-981-3467

Visit:
www.TheRealEstateRenegades.com
or
www.RockStarInnerCircle.com
For articles, tips, opinions, videos and a
FREE Weekly Real Estate Investing
Newsletter that is received by over 20,000
subscribers.

Rob Minton
38238 Glenn Avenue
Willoughby, Ohio 44094
Phone: 440-918-0047
Fax: 440-918-0347

About the Authors

Tom Karadza quit his job as a Software Sales Manager at NetSuite Inc. as it was going public on the New York Stock Exchange (NYSE), to be a full time real estate entrepreneur and investor.

Nick Karadza also quit his job at a Fortune 500 software company, Oracle Corporation, to give real estate 100% of his focus. He began investing at the age of 21 by successfully buying, renovating, and selling a home for profit in only 3 months.

Tom and Nick are real estate professionals that are focused on helping real estate investors in the Greater Toronto Area create income for life. Tom & Nick are active real estate investors themselves, are both registrants with the Real Estate Council of Ontario, and the founders of Rock Star Real Estate Inc. in Oakville, Ontario.

They have been featured in national media such as the National Post, Canadian Real Estate Magazine, the Business News Network, and numerous local publications as well.

Together, Tom and Nick have worked with over 1,000 real estate investors acquiring over 290 million dollars of investment real estate to implement these profitable investing strategies across southern Ontario.

Rob Minton quit his job as a Certified Public Accountant for one of the largest international public accounting firms to be a full-time real estate entrepreneur. He started and built his real estate brokerage from the ground up. Rob's unique approach has made him an in-demand author, speaker, and real estate consultant. For the last 8 years, real estate investors have turned to Rob to create monthly cash flow and wealth in their spare time.